# Reviews of Ov

"This will quickly become the most important book for every employee looking to stay valuable in an increasingly automated world! *Own Your Work Journey* is a powerful guide to honing critical soft skills and learning to stay ahead."

—Dr. Marshall Goldsmith is the Thinkers50 #1 Executive Coach and *New York Times* bestselling author of *The Earned Life, Triggers, and What Got You Here Won't Get You There*

"Ed Hess has earned the right to be called a master teacher, leader, and coach. His past books have built a foundation of wisdom, practical advice, and empirically grounded prescriptions for leadership success and life-skills development. Ed's latest book, *Own Your Work Journey*, is an accumulation of his wisdom over the last several decades. If I were going to trust someone to provide useful guidance and proven advice for guiding one's career and personal life in this era of ubiquitous technology, ambiguity, uncertainty, and rapid change, I would select Ed. Don't pass this one by."

—Kim Cameron, William Russell Kelly Professor Emeritus of Management & Organizations, Ross School of Business, and Professor Emeritus of Higher Education, School of Education, University of Michigan

"Today's world is one where change is the norm and complexity is constantly accumulating. It can be overwhelming at any level. Ed Hess shares a proven array of tools and practices that can help you thrive at work and live that "best life" we all seek."

—George W. Casey, Jr., General, U.S. Army (retired)

"This book will be your best friend. It challenges you to be courageous and "Take Ownership of You" so that you can be an Adaptive Life-long Learner able to navigate the continuous waves of change driven by smart technology. Ed Hess gives you the tools and practices that will help you thrive on your Journey to Best Self. As a social scientist and a person who regularly uses what Ed recommends in my own life, I know this stuff works. This short book is powerful. Buy it! Use it!"

—Jim Detert, John L. Colley Professor at the University of Virginia's Darden School of Business, and author of *Choosing Courage*

"A compelling case for the power of emotional intelligence. 'To learn, unlearn, and relearn at the speed of change,' you must be willing to slow down; learn to challenge what you believe you already know; and be willing to engage yourself and others with reflective listening, humility, and compassion. This workbook provides a roadmap to becoming a vital contributor to the work force in this Age of Smart Technology and teaches you to bring your 'Best Self' to every human interaction."

—Kimberley C. Bassett, Ph.D., Certified Life Coach & Assistant Dean for Undergraduate Academic Advising, Whiting School of Engineering, Johns Hopkins University

"In this amazing guide to survival in the era of exponentially advancing technologies, Ed Hess outlines the basics of human re-invention: how we need to transform ourselves and cope with change. I can't believe how much he has packed into so few pages! This book will help you live happier and healthier lives."

—Vivek Wadhwa, renowned academic, entrepreneur, author, and futurist who in 2018 was awarded Silicon Valley Forum's Visionary Award

"We are living in a time of extraordinary change which will disrupt our life and disorient us at an overwhelming pace. Career patterns and current ways of working no longer will work. Presciently, Ed Hess gives us a clear, concise, and practical approach to meaningfully navigate The Smart Technology Age. Whether keeping your job or taking a new job or managing or leading a workforce in the private or public sector, *Own Your Work Journey* is more than a starting point for what's ahead; it will be the essential and frequent touchstone for personal and professional balance, achievement, and fulfillment in a world awash in change."

—Admiral Gary Roughead, U.S. Navy (Retired), former Chief of Naval Operations

"This wonderful book blends the main lessons of ancient wisdom with state-of-the-art scientific results on how we can become our best selves. It offers a practical roadmap so that we can use our humanity in our favor – not against us – in the smart technological age. It is an essential manual to be read and reread many times by everyone. Give yourself the best gift and own your own journey by following the path Ed himself walked and that he now magnificently provides us with in this book!"

—Dr. Alexandre Di Miceli da Silveira, Professor of Leadership and Business Ethics, founder of Virtuous Company and author of *The Virtuous Barrel*

"*Own Your Work Journey* is a masterpiece 'How-to' and 'Why-to' book! Ed Hess explains the human skills that will be hard for technology to automate and then shares with you best practices to develop those skills. He gives you the tools that will help you take ownership of your ego, mind, body, emotions, behaviors, listening and thinking so you can learn - unlearn and relearn at the speed of change. That is how you can have meaningful work in the Smart Technology Age. I highly recommend this book. It will change your life for the better!"

—Mahan Tavakoli, CEO Strategic Leadership Ventures; Former Board Chair of Leadership Greater, Washington

"This is an amazing book! Its purpose is to help you have meaningful work, and happiness in the Age of Smart Technology. Your success and happiness will depend in large part on how you manage yourself and the choices you make. Don't let technology or other people control your emotions or your thoughts or your behaviors. Own your work life and your non- work life. Ed Hess gives you proven tools to do that."

—Dr. Susan E. Sweeney: Former President, GGB Bearing Technology; Former CHRO & SVP EnPro Industries; Adjunct Professor, College of Business, Wilmington University

"Ed Hess has masterfully summarized what we need to adopt and then apply in our work, our education, and our life. Amazingly, in a world of rapidly evolving smart technology, the skills most valuable are the ones most innately human. Own Your Work Journey not only helps you discover the power-assets in your humanity, but it also charts a behavioral course for you to achieve

– self-actualization – 'Becoming Your Best Self.' That will help you – as technology advances – to have meaningful work. That is not only possible – it's what'll save us all."

—Byron Sanders, President & CEO of BIG THOUGHT – EMPOWERING YOUTH – CLOSING THE OPPORTUNITY GAP

"*Own Your Work Journey* is a powerful roadmap for adults and teens who want to have meaningful work in a world that is rapidly eliminating traditional jobs through technology and automation. I spent most of my career leading industrial companies with large numbers of hourly workers. I know what it takes for workers to become highly adaptive learners. This book gives you the tools and practices to be a highly adaptive learner in the Smart Technology Age. My advice to you is: START TODAY!"

—Steve Macadam, retired Vice Chairman, CEO and President of EnPro Industries, Inc., and serves on the Boards of three public companies

"In this very timely and practical book, Ed Hess lays out an actionable roadmap for how we can bring our best selves to the challenges and opportunities we face in our professional and personal lives. He provides valuable tips, tools, and insights to accompany us on this journey. Ed's energy and passion for unlocking human potential leaps out of every page and exercise. What I love most about this book is that you feel like Ed is personally coaching and inspiring you throughout."

—Craig Dowden (PhD), *Wall Street Journal* and *USA Today* bestselling author of *A Time to Lead: Mastering Your Self... So You Can Master Your World*, Executive Coach and Keynote Speaker

"A life-changing book written by an old soul. Old souls are wise beyond their years, humble, and curious. They see the big picture, feel connected to everything, and recognize their fellow old souls. I feel like an old soul when I read Ed's books. I invite you to enjoy this book and gain wisdom beyond your years."

—Aidan McCullen, Author of *Undisruptable* and Host of *The Innovation Show*

# OWN YOUR
# WORK JOURNEY!

The Path to Meaningful Work
and Happiness in the Age of Smart
Technology & Radical Change!

Edward D. Hess

Cover and text design by Mayapriya Long, Bookwrights
Printed in the United States of America

ISBN 979-8-9874423-0-2  paperback
ISBN 979-8-9874423-1-9  ebook

**This Book is Dedicated to YOU!**

*Its sole purpose is to help you have Meaningful Work & Happiness in the Age of Smart Technology and Radical Change.*

# Contents

# Acknowledgments

I have been very fortunate to have had many people who have had a big positive impact on my journey. Some were teachers, coaches, clients, or bosses. Some were collaborators, friends, or relatives. I am listing them in chronological order — from earliest on. My deepest heartfelt gratitude to:

My Daddy and Mother; Coach Charles Grisham, Sonny Allen, Joe and Terry Street, Ralph Parkman, Coach Ray Graves, Coach Fred Pancoast, Coach Ed Kensler, Brady and Jim, Professor Sydney Jourard, Professor Arthur Combs, Senator Robert Kennedy, Dean Al Turnbull, Dean Monrad Paulson, Professor Antonin Scalia, Professor Charles M. Davison, Jr., Amy Morris Hess, Ira T. Wender, Peter J. Norton, and Jack White.

Professor Lyle Bourne Jr., Katherine Leigh Acuff, David Bonderman, David Schwarz, Tom Aiello, John Schwieters, Terry Brown, Dean Tom Robertson, Professor Robert Drazin, Professor Robert Kazanjian, Professor Jag Sheth, Professor Al Hartgraves, Dean Maryam Alavi, Professor Kim Cameron, Professor Jane Dutton, President Jimmy Carter, Horst Schulte, Herb Kelleher, Tom Cousins, Billy Wren, and Bill Turner.

Dean Robert Bruner, Professor Jeanne Liedtka, Professor Sherwood Frey, Professor Ed Davis, Professor Bob Landel, Professor John Colley, Professor Sankaran Venkataraman, Dr. Sean Carr, Professor Richard D'Aveni, Professor Bill Fulmer, Professor Jim Detert, Professor Tom Steenburgh, Cassy Eriksson, Katherine Ludwig, and Ray Dalio.

# Introduction

## Who is Ed?

To connect with you, I want to give you a good feel for who I am. I will share with you the obstacles that I overcame in my life and how I came to wholeheartedly own my journey.

Everything that I recommend in this book that you do—I have done!

My life story has had these consistent themes.

### I'm an Outsider. I have never been a member of the in-crowd.

I came from a very humble background. I was raised in rural Georgia where my parents were considered outsiders. My father was an immigrant, and my mother was from Massachusetts. They were different than almost all the people living there. I was the only boy in my elementary school class who went out for the peewee football team and was not chosen to be on the team—in a town where football was king. I was chubby. I wore the wrong blue jeans. I was not an athlete. I never had a high school girlfriend.

### I have always been a non-traditional player and explorer.

That means I have excelled at many different jobs for which I did not have the formal training. I was trained professionally to be a lawyer, but I have had four very different, successful careers. I was able to do this because I was realistic—I knew what I did not know. And I knew how to learn. And I had learned that it was ok to say, "I don't know."

My first big job at a global investment banking firm involved taking companies public and raising private equity. I told the Chairman of the firm that I did not know how to do a simple IRR (internal rate of return) computation. He responded: "I know you well and I know you know how to learn, and I bet you will know how to do an IRR by the end of the weekend." And I did!

I learned to be an explorer in my childhood, reading books about successful people—athletes, leaders, doctors—and dreaming about leaving the rural country and going to the big city to become a successful person. That fueled my love of going into the unknown and figuring out what to do. That way of living is still with me today. I still am an avid reader — that is how I learn. I work hard to stay relevant in our crazy world.

## Be Courageous.

My father was a courageous man and he taught me to be courageous. My working life has mostly involved having the courage to go into the unknown and figure things out. That was how I have been able to live a life very different from what was expected. I grew up wanting to be courageous so he would be proud of me. That was the compelling story I created as to why I needed to be courageous, to overcome my fears, and to help others be courageous too.

## Stand Up for Yourself.

When I took a training course to become a lifeguard, the trainer was much older and bigger than me, and he was much harsher with me than he was with any other trainee. During a training session, he once held me underwater so long that I almost drowned and he had to lift me out of the pool and lay me on the sidewalk. No other trainee that day was treated that way. He told me I flunked. When I went home and told my father I was not going to be a lifeguard, he said: "Son, you can't be a quitter so give it one more try, and if it does not work then move on. And if he tries to drown you again, kick him as hard as you can in his 'balls.'" I followed my father's advice, and I became a lifeguard.

I had three other instances in my work life when someone treated me unfairly or discriminated against me. Each time, I called them out and demanded they take action to make it right. I am talking about *big bads* that could have negatively impacted my life and career. I am not talking about insults or mistakes. I stood up to powerful people and they all made amends.

## The Power of Others.

Many times, in my life Others have opened doors for me by giving me opportunities to become far more than I ever dreamed I could be. Ways that completely transformed my life trajectory. People saw something in me that generated their kindness and trust. That can happen to you, too, if you approach the world with a positive mindset, the right behaviors, and a willingness to learn and work hard and well with others.

May I share an example with you?

Football was king in rural Georgia, and the summer before I started high school, a legendary coach named Charles Grisham asked me if I wanted to be a Student Athletic Trainer for the football team. I never had met him, and to this day, I don't know how he found me or why he made the offer he did. At that time, I knew nothing about being an athletic trainer, but I said yes anyway because I was not afraid of failure.

Then he did something that changed my and my familys'

life in that small town. (Remember, my family and I were out-siders.). He said: "I want you to come to my house every school day at 7:30 am, and I will take you to school with me." So, for the next five years, I rode to school sitting shotgun next to the best football coach in Western Georgia. You can't imagine how much his friendship and generosity positively impacted the rest of the community's treatment of me and my family.

In short, Coach Grisham changed my life. He went on to help me publish my first authored article at the age of 17 in Coach & Athlete magazine; he made me his first base coach on the baseball team, and he helped me get a full football scholar-ship as a Student Athletic Trainer at the University of Florida.

To this day, I thank and express my love to him and Mrs. Grisham every morning in my gratitude meditation practice. I am who I am today because of his kindness, help, and generous spirit.

Over my life span I have had over 25 other "angels" – people who saw something in me and gave me opportunities to learn and flourish. I have been very fortunate – you can be very fortu-nate, too.

Be the type of person that Others will want to help. Work hard. Be a learner. Have integrity. Help others.

## Have the Courage to Ask.

Many times, I have reached out to prominent people whom I did not know and asked for their help. My ask was usually in the form of an email or a letter, which succinctly set out who I was and my reasons for reaching out to them—my compelling "why." I was a good storyteller, and I was honest. I did not blow smoke. I very rarely had anyone turn me down.

That is how my wife and I were the first marriage ceremony that Supreme Court Justice Ruth Bader Ginsburg performed when she was named a DC Federal Circuit Court of Appeals Judge.

That is how I got the opportunity to write the first extensive public story about Ray Dalio and his company Bridgewater Associates—a 54-page chapter in my Learn or Die book.

Having the courage to tell my story is also how I got accepted into the University of Virginia Law School in May of 1968 after the incoming Class for that September was already chosen. I had not filed an application or taken the Law School Admission Test. I called the Law School and asked to talk to the Dean. His Assistant answered the phone and asked me why I wanted to talk to him. I told her my story which included the fact that I very recently had decided I wanted to go to Law School after meeting United States Senator Robert Kennedy that spring. The Dean took my call and after having a 45-minute conversation with me, he said; "Son, I will see you here in September. You are accepted."

Early in my first year of Law School I initiated a change in the dress code at UVA Law School with the help of a new Dean. At the UVA Law School, a coat and tie were required daily, and we went to school six days a week. Well, you know I came from a humble background. I did not own a coat. So, before going to Law School my parents took me into Atlanta and bought me one very nice suit. I wore that suit—the same suit—to class every day for months. Since we went to school on Saturdays, I could not get that one suit dry cleaned.

So here I was a poor student who was having to answer other students' questions about why I wore the same suit every day. It was embarrassing. So, what did I do? I had the courage to request an appointment with the Dean.

He accepted my request and started off the conversation by

asking me why I wanted to see him. I told him "You are discriminating against poor people by having your coat and tie policy." Obviously, that took him by surprise and being a renown Poverty Law scholar, he was very sensitive to that allegation. So, I told him my story. I told him my background. I told him why I came to his Law School. I told him how it felt to have other students continually ask me why I wore the same suit every day. He listened. He said, "Come back and see me on Monday."

Well, on Monday morning as I was walking towards the school, I noticed a large crowd on the steps waiting to get inside the building. I got in line. I finally got to read the framed announcement by the door to the Dean's Office: "Effective today, a coat and tie will no longer required at the UVA Law School."

## Read Books!

My family had very limited money. Nonetheless, my mother saved a little money every week and every couple of months she took me and my little brother to the only bookstore in our town and let us buy two books to read. I chose books about famous people or sports heroes. Books enabled my dreams. Books were how I learned possibilities — there are lots of different ways to be successful and happy.

Reading was how I learned to love learning and exploring.

I shared these themes in my life for three reasons:

1. To help you understand that you can take control of your life and that you can be the type of person that others will want to help.

2. To show you that an outsider like me—a person not part of the in crowd—can have a good life with the help of others.

3. To share with you the some of the behaviors that will help you be more than you think you can be.

Others played a big role in helping me become who I am.

We all need Others to help us be all we can be.

We all need to be the type of person Others will want to help.

# 📋 Workshop #1

Please write down your answers to these two questions:

*1. What are your life goals?*

*2. How would you define the good life?*

*Did you have any of these thoughts:*

- Have a good job?
- Have a good marriage?
- Have a good family?
- Have good friends?
- Be successful?
- Raise good children?
- Earn a good living?
- Live a meaningful life?
- Be happy?

Your being able to do those things is highly dependent upon the person you are — the person who you bring to the game of life each day.

This book is all about how you can take ownership of you — ownership of who you are and ownership of how you live your life so that you can achieve your goals.

Ownership of how you think, listen, learn, and relate to

others. Ownership of your ego, mind, body, emotions, words, and behaviors.

The purpose of this book is to help you *Own Your Life* including *Own Your Work Life*. Owning your work life will help you achieve your life goals.

We all are entering a new era — a new time — a whole new game driven by Smart Technology and Radical Change. Technology will become smarter and smarter and will automate tens of millions of jobs. The pace of change will become faster and faster requiring all of us to continuously learn new skills so we can have meaningful work and happiness achieving our life goals.

.. .. .. .. .. .. .. .. .. .. .. .. .. .. .. ..

# The Who – The Why –The How

I wrote this book for every person 18 years old or older who wants to:

- Have meaningful work and live a happy life.
- Be successful and respected as a unique human being.
- Not be left behind or overwhelmed by the pace of continual technological, economic, and social change in an era of radical change, social divisiveness, and climate change.
- Not be automated out of a job by artificial intelligence or smart robots within the coming decades.

Achieving those goals is highly dependent upon how you think, listen, behave, manage your emotions, relate to and collaborate with others, and learn, unlearn, and relearn at the speed of change.

The guidance in this book can be used by every human being 18 years or older of every race, color, physical appearance, religion or non-religion, sexual orientation, income level, and education level.

The ability to *Own Your Work Journey* is not dependent upon the grades you made in school, or the status you have in society, or the amount of money you earn, or the number of followers you have on social media, or the brand of clothing you wear, or the type of vehicle you drive, or how you look.

This book is for every human being. It matters not what your job is — the lessons apply to all of us — to the worker on the factory floor, to the service worker, to hourly workers, to self-employed workers, to doctors and nurses, to lawyers, to professionals, to entrepreneurs, and to the managers and executives of companies. No one will be exempt from the changes that technology will create.

You will live in the most disruptive domestic time since the Great Depression. What got you here won't get you there in this new era of constant change and upheaval.

**The purpose of this book is to help you OWN YOUR WORK JOURNEY!**

**The foundational building block of *Own Your Work Journey* is you becoming your *Best Self.***

**Your goal is to learn how to bring your Best Self to your world every day. That is the pathway to meaningful work and happiness.**

To be your Best Self requires you to take control of your life by taking ownership of your ego, your mind, your emotions, your body, and your words and behaviors so you can continuously learn and adapt to the pace of change.

That will enable you to continually think and listen better, make better decisions, generate positive emotions, manage your negative emotions, be more productive, and have positive relationships with others. Those are the skills that are necessary to navigate and have a happy life in this new era.

**The Journey to your Best Self will give you the tools to help you overcome your insecurities, and fears — which everyone has—so you can be more resilient and make better life choices and decisions and behave in ways that will bring you happiness without hurting others.**

# THE WHY

*Why do you need to be on a Journey to your Best Self?*

- Because technology is going to continue to transform how you live and how you work and determine in large part whether you will have work.

- The Smart Technology Age will be an age of constant change that will require you to continually adapt and continuously learn new skills to have good jobs.

- Technology will continue to advance in many areas: artificial intelligence, biotechnology, nanotechnology, genetic engineering, virtual and augmented reality, human-like robots, 3D Printing, digital medicine, imbedding technology in your body, flying cars, and powerful drones, etc.  All of this is likely in the next 10 years!

- Technology is going to become more *human* because it will be able to do many tasks that we humans are now paid to do.

- Technology will automate blue- and white-collar jobs. In all cases, technology is going to take over doing the work that many of us do now.

- The best research from Oxford University predicts that between 25-47% of the U.S. workforce will be automated by the end of this decade. Millions of jobs will be automated.

**Jobs generally predicted to be automated include:** customer service jobs, banking jobs, taxi drivers, long-haul truck drivers, bus drivers, data entry people, accountants, auditors, assembly and factory workers, travel agents, market researchers, telemarketers, couriers, business managers, bookkeepers, typists, cashiers, retail sales people, radiologists, librarians, loan officers, delivery of small parcels, and data-based jobs that involve doing the same tasks over and over again.

Having the same job working for the same employer for five years or more will be history for most people. The best scientists predict that the average person will have five completely different jobs in the coming decades.

**That means all of us will need to continually update our skills and/or learn new skills.** Thinking and learning skills will be very important. As will be emotional skills. All of us will need to constantly improve those skills in order to have jobs.

The other big technology challenge for all of us is preventing technology from hacking our emotions—influencing how we feel, how we behave, and how we define ourselves.

**You will need to *Own Your Journey* — because YOU will not be happy being a human puppet manipulated or put out of work by technology.**

**You can't stay the same as you are now. You will have to continually adapt as the world adapts.**

**Your biggest competition going forward is not other people—it's YOU!**

Life will become more hectic and more challenging for all of us in the Age of Smart Technology and Radical Change. That means you will need to excel at learning, unlearning, and relearning at the pace of change. I call that *Hyper-Learning*. This book gives you the tools to do that.

**You and I will have work if we can do the tasks that add value in ways that technology can't add value.** At least for the foreseeable future, there are three ways for us to do that:

1. Thinking in ways different from smart technology's way of thinking. Those ways are higher-order critical thinking; making moral judgments; going into the unknown and figuring things out; creative,

imaginative, and innovative thinking; and making decisions in situations where there is lots of uncertainty and not a lot of data.

2. Excelling at building caring, trusting, positive emotional relationships with other human beings, including teammates, customers, co-workers, patients, and clients. This will be your big differentiator from technology.

3. Excelling at doing trade jobs that require human dexterity and iterative diagnostic definitions of the problem and iterative trial- and-error approaches to solving the problem.

**The largest number of human jobs will likely be those service jobs that require positive emotional engagement with other human beings.**

**Ultimately, it will be positive emotional engagement with other humans that will differentiate us from the technology.**

Unfortunately, very few people have learned how to manage their emotions: how to generate positive emotions and how to manage negative emotions.

# Workshop #2:

**Let's take a break here and begin our Workshop — Journaling Practice, which will be key practice for how you will learn and hold yourself accountable.**

» I would like for you to reread the above three types of jobs that have the lowest possibility of being automated and answer these questions:

» Which of those types of jobs are you prepared to do today?

> » Which do you have the training to do?
> » Which do you think you could do if you got the right training?
> » Which of those job(s) would you like to do?

How well we accomplish those tasks that technology won't be able to do well (for the near future) depends upon how well we manage and optimize what's going on inside of us with respect to our ego, our mind, our body, and our emotions.

How well we do that will determine the quality of our thinking, listening, learning, decision making, and our abilities to emotionally connect with others .

Unfortunately, very few of us have been taught how to manage our ego, our mind, our body, our emotions, or our behaviors. That is the challenge for most of us regardless of our education level and our success to date.

The good news is that every person has the capacity to do this. You do not need a college degree. You do not need to be the smartest person in the room.

**You do need to have the self-discipline and the commitment to become your *Best Self.* That is how you will Own Your Journey. The purpose of this book is to help you learn how to do that!**

. .. .. .. .. .. .. .. .. .. .. .. ..

# THE HOW

**This is a how-to book.**

**It is a learn-by-doing book.**

**It is a create-your-new-story book.**

In this book, I will ask you lots of questions to help you *Own Your Journey.*

You will be much more successful if you adopt the Daily Practices that I will share with you.

**I will ask you to write down your answers to questions or requests in a personal workbook or journal or on your tech device so you will have in one place all your learnings and your game plan for how you want to go forward to achieve your goals.**

**Through stories, exercises, and suggested daily practices, this book can help you achieve the following:**

**A new way of being that will help you have a happy life with meaningful work and meaningful relationships.**

- Be a better person, a better friend, a better parent, a better learner, a more adaptive person, and a better teammate or colleague.

- Define and develop skills for achieving your version of success.

- Learn how to Own Your Journey and become your Best Self.

- Use Daily Practices that will help achieve the foregoing.

- Learn that your happiness will depend on the type of person you are and not on the number of followers you have on social media or the amount of stuff you have, or on seeing life as a survival-of-the-fittest competition.

- Understand why your biggest human competition will be you, and that you will need the help of others to be your Best Self.

- That is how you can Own Your Journey!

Here are three quotes from great philosophers from my book, *Make It Happen*[1]:

*"Nothing can bring you peace but yourself."*

~ Ralph Waldo Emerson

*"Happiness depends upon ourselves."*  ~ Aristotle

*"The man (and woman) who makes everything that leads to happiness depend upon him (or her) self and not upon other men (or women) has adapted the best plan for living happily."*                     ~Plato

. .. .. .. .. .. .. .. .. .. .. .. .. ..

# 🔖 WORKSHOP #3:

**People learn best by *making meaning* of the words they read.**

*Making Meaning* comes about by writing down what the words mean to you. What did the words say to you? That is the beginnings of you creating your personal story of how you will begin to Own Your Journey in this new era.

Please reread this Chapter and write down your beginning answers to these questions:

1.  Why do I need to Own My Journey and be on my Journey to Best Self?

2.  Which of these 4 Goals feel right for you — please list them in order of your priority starting with #1:

    > Have meaningful work and live a happy life.

    > Be successful and respected as a unique human being.

    > Not be left behind or overwhelmed by the pace of continuous   technological, economic, and social change in an era of radical change, social divisiveness, and climate change.

    > Not be automated out of a job by artificial

intelligence or smart robots within the coming decades.

3. "Your biggest competition going forward is not other people—it's YOU."

> What does that statement mean to you?

> Why is it true?

What did the 3 philosophers' statements above say to you?

# YOU ARE UNIQUE

**You are a unique person. There is only one of you.**

**How about giving yourself a big hug right now?**

**How about say to yourself:**

- *I want to be my best self with my family, my friends, and the world in which I live and work.*

- *I want to be successful—I want to have meaningful work.*

- *I want to be happy.*

How about say to yourself every day when you first wakeup:

- *"I have the potential to be happy, to live a meaningful life with meaningful work and meaningful relationships, and make my unique, positive contribution to the World."*

The Smart Technology Age will require all of us to create a new story that enables us to prosper in a very different environment.

A key part of that story is the need for all of us to *Own Your Journey!*

**Do you really own yourself now?**

**Or have you given that power to other people and/or to technology?**

Becoming your Best Self is the result of *Own Your Journey*, ownership of how you think, how you listen, how you relate to others, how you behave, how you lean, how you adapt, and how you manage your ego, mind, body, and emotions.

**What makes this book different is its behavioral approach.**

**Good intent is necessary, but it is not enough.**

**It all comes down to how you behave.**

The ways to become your *Best Self* are rooted in decades of modern science and thousands of years of teachings of the great ancient Eastern and Western philosophies and the teachings of the seven great religions of the world. We will explore those ways together.

What is so interesting is that modern science, the great philosophies, and the great religions all come to similar conclusions about what it takes to excel as a human being and to find meaning, purpose, and happiness in life.

Here is the formula — the pathway — the game plan:

**To have a meaningful life, meaningful work, meaningful relationships, and happiness requires you to become your Best Self.**

**To become your Best Self requires you to Own Your Journey!**

That is the path I am going to share with you and invite you to embrace!

# 📋 Workshop #4:

Please write down your learnings from this Chapter. What was new? What surprised you? How did it feel? Did it help you understand the purpose of this book?

. .. .. .. .. .. .. .. .. .. .. .. .. .. .. .. .

**CHAPTER**

# What's the Big Challenge?

**The big challenge is us. My big challenge is me. Your big challenge is you.**

Why is that so?

Well, our brains are wired for efficiency and to save energy.

To attain that efficiency, our brains are primed to process incoming information in a way that:

- Confirms what you already believe.
- Affirms your ego — your story about yourself and how your world works.
- Seeks a cohesive story of who we are and how our lives should be.

Our thoughts, emotions, and perceptions all stem from these predictions.

Our brains are not wired to be Hyper-Learners: to learn, unlearn and relearn at the speed of change.

Up to now, our brain's predictions are correct enough to keep us alive and well. But they are not always on the mark. In other words, all of us are predisposed to confirm and affirm, not continually learn and adapt.

# 📋 Workshop #5:

Please write down what those scientific findings about the brain say to you about you. What do the words mean to you? How do they influence your thinking? Your ability to learn? Your ability to adapt?

.. .. .. .. .. .. .. .. .. .. .. .. .. ..

*The science of adult learning is clear—we all are suboptimal learners.*

*We all generally seek to confirm, affirm, and maintain our stories of how our world works.*

**Well, in the Smart Technology Age, that will be the quickest pathway to being automated or unemployed because the speed of change will require all of us to learn at a pace much faster than we ever have had to learn before.**

We all will have to excel at learning, unlearning, and relearning! I call that Hyper-Learning.

That means we will need to think differently.

The good news is we all can take steps to *rewire* ourselves to become a better learner. That is one of the key purposes of this book. The rest of the Chapters in this book are designed to help you learn how to think, learn, listen, adapt, and collaborate in ways that will help you have meaningful work and happiness in this fast-paced technologically driven-world.

Let's stop. Please slowly say out loud three times:

1. "I am a suboptimal learner and I want to be a much better learner!"

2. "I want to have meaningful work and not be unemployable!"

How did that feel? Weird? Good? Not Sure? Do you really believe that?

It is hard for people to say those words. I once invited 50 European Chief Technology Officers I was working with to say out loud, "I am a suboptimal learner." Not one person could say it. Not one.

Why is it so hard to say it? Because most of us do not know how our brain works.

The human brain is amazing. It is made up of over 120 billion neurons and trillions of neuronal connections that are talking to each other 24 hours a day by sending electrical signals and releasing chemicals that create your emotions and responses.

The human brain only weighs about three to four pounds, but it uses about 25% of your body energy. Its evolutionary purpose is to keep you alive. An adult brain matures around age 25. But it can keep learning after that. It has plasticity. It can change.

Our brains learn from past experiences to predict our future needs and it initiates our thoughts, feelings, and perceptions before we are even consciously aware of a particular stimuli or situation.

That means we usually operate on autopilot a lot.

We do not take the time to evaluate what we believe.

We do not slow down and take the time to think about our answer.

We do not slow down and manage our emotions.

That is why we see what we believe rather than the reverse!

That is why we are not that open-minded. That is why we tend to  think we are right, and the other person is wrong.

We all need to learn how to test our thinking. We need to continually ask ourselves questions like:

"Why do I believe this?" "What data would prove I am mistaken?" Have I looked for that information?"

We all will have to learn how to think more like scientists and be very fact and data driven.

Our brains and our bodies are integrally linked. Your brain receives sensory signals from different parts of your body and quickly predicts what those sensations mean based on your stories, past experiences, and beliefs.

In most cases the answers pop up in our minds and we act upon them without really thinking. Scientists have discovered that we have dozens of biases—such as confirmation bias or availability bias—which is the result of the brain's fast predictions.

The good news is that we can change our brain's wiring by managing our thinking, emotions, and body reactions. By challenging and unpacking our assumptions, beliefs, and stories, we can teach our brains to make better predictions based on better information. We can do that by intentionally looking for disconfirming information and evaluating it.

That is very important because the Smart Technology Age we are living in now is an era of fast-paced change, which will challenge our abilities to stay current, to stay relevant, and to stay employed

We all must learn how to learn, unlearn, and relearn at the speed of change.

Living in this new era means that our current stories about how the world works and how we can be successful will not work as well. We all need a new story.

Your mind is your storyteller. We all have our unique

stories about how the world works based on our past experiences, our upbringing, and the culture in which we were raised.

Your mind talks to you a lot. It is making sure you do not go too far afield. Your talking mind is a chatterbox that constantly critiques you or raises issues. The Buddhist philosophers call the mind a "monkey mind" because it is rarely quiet.

Your monkey mind can inhibit learning and you being open minded, and it makes it hard for you to truly listen and understand what others are really saying.

And it gets worse. **The two biggest inhibitors to learning are your ego and your fears.** Your ego gets in the way of learning because it thinks you are always right. Your fears of not being liked, looking stupid, being wrong, or making mistakes further inhibit learning

**Emotionally we are wired to be defensive listeners and thinkers.** When someone disagrees with us or has views different than us, our usual automatic response is to deny, defend, or deflect—the 3 Ds.

And many of us let our emotions get the best of us. I remember early in my marriage, my wife, who is much smarter than me in many areas, and I were having a debate about something that was getting heated because I knew I was right. I started to get emotional and that changed my tone and volume of my talking.

When that happened, she said: "Let's calm down for a minute. You know that you can control how you behave and there is not an automatic link between your emotions and your behaviors."

I responded: "No, I did not know that." And she said: "Well, you need to slow yourself down. Take a deep breath or two before you automatically raise your voice because it is not a loving way to respond."

And she was right.

How do you adapt to this new era?

You need to **Own Your Journey**!

You need to **Take Ownership of YOU**: your ego, your mind, your thinking, your body, your emotions, your words, your behaviors, how you listen and how you communicate with other human beings.

Doing that will lead you to be a much better learner, thinker, listener, decision-maker, and collaborator. A much better person —one who can adapt better and continuously learn as technology changes the world.

It will also enable you to be an explorer and have the courage to go into the unknown and figure things out.

It will enable you to build positive emotional relationship with others.

**That is how you will have the best possibility of having meaningful work, meaningful personal relationships, and happiness in a world dominated by Smart Technology and Radical Change.**

# 📋 Workshop #6

Please review this chapter and write down your story about the *Science of You* — What does the science say about how you think, listen, learn, and relate to others? What does that mean to you?

Will your current way of being help you thrive in the Smart Technology Era?

What can you do to have a better chance of having meaningful work and happiness in the Age of Smart Technology?

. .. .. .. .. .. .. .. .. .. .. .. .. ..

# 📋 Workshop #7

## WHO ARE YOU?

**Own Your Journey begins with you understanding who you are right now. Please answer the following sets of questions truthfully in your Journal.**

Answer truthfully with yes or no:

- Do you give others the power to define who you are?
- Do you let others determine your happiness?
- Do you let social media influence how you feel about yourself?
- Do believe you can make your life better?
- Do you look forward to each day as an opportunity?
- Do you have many days that are hard to get through?
- Do you believe your life options are very limited?
- Do you fear change?
- I really can't do much to change my life.
- I am generally afraid to try new things.
- I would like to have more control over my life.
- I would like to feel better about myself.
- I want to be successful.
- I want to be a better person.
- I know how to become a better person.
- I want to have meaningful work.
- I have meaningful work now.

- I want to have meaningful relationships.
- I want to be happier.

**Be honest and please write out your answers to these questions in your Journal:**

- What makes me feel happy?
- What makes me feel unhappy?
- What am I good at doing?
- What do I find hard to do?
- How would I define Meaningful Work and what would it looklike?
- How would I define a Meaningful Relationship and what would that look like?
- So far in my life, what am I most proud of doing?
- So far in my life, what am I disappointed about?

Answering those questions truthfully will help you. There are no wronganswers. The answers will help you focus on what you need to improve. That is why we are here together. To help you be all you can be!

In the next chapter we will explore the big obstacles everyone must face to become their *Best Self* along with ways to overcome those obstacles.

.. .. .. .. .. .. .. .. .. .. .. .. .. .. .. ..

# Quiet Your Ego

In Chapter 2, we discussed the science of adult learning—how we are wired to seek confirmation of what we already believe and how we seek to affirm our ego—our stories about ourselves and how our world works.

And we learned that the two big inhibitors to being able to learn new things and new ways of working are our ego and our fears.

To continually learn and adapt at the pace of change, we all need to overcome our ego and our fears. In this chapter, we are going to focus on developing a quiet ego.

Developing a quiet ego is foundational to becoming your Best Self and bringing your Best Self to the world each day so you can have meaningful work, meaningful relationships, and happiness in a world characterized by fast-paced, continuous change and automation of jobs.

## Workshop #8

### WHAT IS A QUIET EGO?

**Please write down your answers to these questions:**

- Is a quiet ego the opposite of a big ego?
- You must know people with a big ego. In fact, you

may know a lot of people with a big ego. What about them says to you that they have a big ego?

**Please write down a list of observable behaviors that would evidence to you that the person has a BIG EGO.**

What did you come up with?

Now how about ask two close friends to describe how a person with a big ego behaves?

Please take your list and your two friends' lists and make a summary list of how a person with a big ego would likely behave.

Here's how I would describe someone with a big ego:

# BIG EGO PEOPLE

- Loves being the center of attention.
- Tends to take over or dominate the conversation.
- Must be right.
- Always defend their ideas rigorously.
- Rarely asks questions. They excel at *telling*.
- Frequently interrupt people who are talking.
- Loves bragging about their accomplishments.
- Rarely says: "I am wrong."
- Rarely says: "I don't know."
- Seeks or want praise.
- Interrupts people to tell them they are wrong.
- Focuses on looking good to others.
- Sucks up to their boss.
- Rarely says thank you.
- Rarely asks other people how they're feeling.
- Don't truly listen (they multitask).

- Rarely apologize to others.
- Rarely ask others for help.
- Often says they are better than others.
- Intentionally puts down people—trying to make them look bad or inferior or stupid.

. .. .. .. .. .. .. .. .. .. .. .. .. ..

# 📋 Workshop #9

Please take your list, your friends' lists, and my list of Big Ego People's characteristics and behaviors and write down in your Journal the opposite or inverse of those behaviors that might define a Quiet Ego.

I love this exercise. It is so much fun. Think about it — the reverse or the opposite of a bad behavior is a good behavior.

Now you have a behavioral definition of a Quiet Ego.

Now you have a roadmap of how a person with a Quiet Ego behaves.

Now you can choose the Quiet Ego behaviors that you don't do enough or well and start to work on improving one to two of those behaviors. We will discuss how to do that in a future chapter.

Why is having a Quiet Ego so important?

In your Journal, please complete the following statements:

- A quiet ego makes it more likely that I will behave in the following ways: _____.
- Those new ways of behaving will enable me to do the following things better: _____.

Then please take a short break.

**Welcome back!**

Here are some examples of answers to the exercise you just did. These are not the only answers. And I am not saying your examples are wrong. These might be some you hadn't thought of.

- A quiet ego enables me to be more open minded so I will not be so defensive if my views are challenged.

- A quiet ego helps me to be fully present so I can listen better to other peoples' views, and that helps me understand what they are saying so I can learn from them.

- A quiet ego enables me to change my views if someone has a better answer or approach.

- A quiet ego helps me be a better collaborator.

- A quiet ego helps me be less defensive and that helps me ask questions so I can learn.

- A quiet ego helps me focus on what is right and not on who is right.

- A quiet ego helps me actively critique my beliefs or positions so that I will not make mistakes.

# HOW DO YOU ACHIEVE A QUIET EGO?

How do you start to develop a quiet ego?

The answer brings into play the science of deliberate practice—a process for changing your story and improving your behaviors.

The research of renowned cognitive psychologists Anders Ericsson, Lyle Bourne, Jr., and Alice Healy showed that:

**Learning something new or improving a skill requires daily deliberate practice in small bits or chunks and that you are more likely to be successful if you do it daily and**

**hold yourself accountable by measuring yourself daily.**

Professor Ericsson developed a theory of expertise based on deliberate practice, while Professors Bourne and Healy focused on the best ways to train people to learn new things. In full disclosure, Dr. Bourne was my graduate psychology advisor and has been my *anam cara* (soul friend) for over four decades.

**Regarding measuring yourself, people have found it very helpful to have an Accountability Partner. An Accountability Partner is someone whom you can trust who will give you honest, caring feedback frequently.**

Share with your Accountability Partner the behaviors you are trying to improve or eliminate and give them the *power* to give you feedback real time without you asking them.

And when they do, please thank them, and then pause and reflect — do not automatically use the 3D's: Deny, Defend, or Deflect.

In the next chapter we will explore four proven practices that you can use to help you develop a quiet ego.

.. .. .. .. .. .. .. .. .. .. .. .. .. .. ..

# Taking Ownership of You!

## Are You Ready?

# Let's Start Your Journey!

CHAPTER

# Quiet Your Ego Practices!

We all have an ego.

Your ego is your story about yourself—who you are—and how you want others to view you.

We all automatically react in ways that defend our story.

Everyone wants to look smart; to be well thought of; to be better than other people. That is how many people think—we think we are better than other people.

**When our story is challenged most of us automatically respond with one or more of the 3 D's: we deny; we defend; and we deflect.**

You have learned in earlier chapters that the science of adult learning clearly shows that our stories are not always right or correct. In fact, they are rarely correct because we are wired to seek confirmation of what we already believe; affirmation of our ego; and to defend our story about how our world works.

So, we need to create a new story that will better serve us as we go forward in a world characterized now by smart technology, social divisiveness, job volatility, and political instability.

**We need to create a new story that includes adaptability and the need to continuously learn, unlearn and relearn at the pace of change in order to stay relevant in the workplace.**

# HUMILITY—THE NEW SUCCESS STORY

Unfortunately, in the United States, many people—especially men think practicing or showing humility indicates weakness. This is based on a misunderstanding of the concept.

My dear friend and mentor, Professor Kim Cameron in his wonderful book *Positively Energizing Leadership* states that:

**"Humility is esteemed by all the major religions and philosophies as a cardinal virtue."** [2]

Think about that — all the major religions and philosophies espouse that Humility is a cardinal virtue. What does that say to you? Is Humility a good thing? Is Humility a great thing?

Psychologist June Price Tangey has defined the psychological attributes of humility as:

1. *Having an accurate (not over or underestimated) view of one's abilities and achievements.*

2. *Being able to acknowledge one's mistakes, imperfections, gaps in knowledge, and limitations.*

3. *Being open to new ideas, contradictory information, and advice.*

4. *Keeping one's abilities and accomplishments in perspective.*

5. *Having a low focus on self or a tendency to "forget the self."*

6. *Appreciating the value of all things and the many ways other people and things contribute to the world.* [3]

Those 6 attributes define humility.

# 📋 Workshop #10

Please read each of those six above attributes again slowly and think about each one.

In your Journal, please write down your answers to these questions:

- How would each of the six humility attributes help you have a quiet ego?
- How would you behave so that your behaviors would evidence those six attributes?

Did you include any of the following behaviors?

- I will be less defensive.
- When someone disagrees with me, I will not react negatively. I will seek to understand why they disagree.
- I will demonstrate an open mind and curiosity by asking questions and not being defensive if someone disagrees with me.
- I will ask questions to understand, and I will seek to learn not to just confirm my views.
- I will freely admit when I am wrong.
- I will ask myself why do I believe what I believe.
- I will look for information that would disconfirm my beliefs.
- I will respect and try to understand different views or approaches.
- I will freely say "I don't know" when I don't know.

Please take a break now and let the humility discussion settle in your mind and your heart.

. .. .. .. .. .. .. .. .. .. .. .. .. ..

OK! Let's keep going—it gets better!!

**The mediocrity principle also aligns with the psychological attributes of humility.**

It was defined this way by biologist P.Z. Myers:

*"The mediocrity principle simply states that you aren't that special."*

*"The universe does not revolve around you...Most of what happens in the world is just a consequence of natural, universal laws — laws that apply everywhere and to everything."*[4]

Wow, you aren't that special. The universe does not revolve around you.

I know I am not that special. Do you think you are that special?

I know the universe does not revolve around me. Do you think the universe revolves around you?

How about say out loud: "I am not that special." Was it easy to say?

Do you believe it? How did it feel?

What does that mean to you?

Does the universe revolve around you? Of course not.

Well, a person with a big ego believes it does.

Yes, you are unique. No one else is like you.

Does that make you special?

Well, it makes you different!

Does that mean that everyone you meet should think you are special?

Well, everyone should respect your human dignity and you should respect theirs.

But does that mean you are better than them?

No, believing that you are better paves the way to a big ego.

A big ego forces you to see life as a competition — everyone else is competitor unless they agree with you.

**Well, please let me be the first person to inform you that your biggest competition in the Smart Technology Age will be yourself!**

Yes, your biggest competition will be you because you will have to continuously improve yourself and learn new skills as smart technology advances and automates more jobs.

**Humility is all about:**

- **Not being so self-centered.**
- **Having an open mind.**
- **Accepting your strengths, weaknesses, and mistakes.**
- **Keeping your abilities and accomplishments in perspective.**
- **Appreciating others.**
- **Seeking to learn and improve every day.**

**To have humility is to believe that "it's not all about me."**

Embracing humility enables you to tamp down your defensiveness and competitiveness with others.

You don't have to get defensive.

You just need to be a better learner and a better person each day.

Having humility means being able to say:

- "I don't know"

- "That is a good point—I had not thought about that. Thank you."
- "Can you help me? I am having trouble doing or understanding this."

With humility, you can listen to another person in a non-judgmental, caring manner.

With humility you can recognize what you do not know and figure out how to learn what you need to know.

In her book *The Joy in Loving: A Guide to Daily Living*, Mother Teresa put forth some practices to enable humility, and I have taken the liberty to paraphrase them as follows:

> Speak as little as possible about yourself

> Mind your own business—don't voluntarily judge or critique others

> Don't try to manage other people's lives

> Accept valid corrections cheerfully

> Respect the human dignity of others

What do you think of those five statements?

Should you consider adopting them?

Some years ago, I created a Behavioral Diagnostic for business and military leaders. I have used that diagnostic with thousands of leaders and managers. And what do you think was the number one behavior that needed to be improved?

The #1 behavior that nearly everyone needed to improve was HUMILITY.

. .. .. .. .. .. .. .. .. .. .. .. .. ..

# 📋 Workshop #11

**Please review this Chapter again — it is that important!**

**Then, please answer the following question in your Journal:**

1. **"Embracing and behaving in ways that evidence humility would help me do or be what ????"**

Yes, I am asking you to please make a list of all the ways adopting humility as a key behavior would help you be on your Journey to Best Self!

―――

Did your List include the following points?

Here is what practicing humility enables and makes easier.

- A Quiet Ego.
- Thinking in ways that Smart Technology won't be able to do well.
- Truly listening to learn from others in a nonjudgmental, non-defensive manner.
- Learning from others and making better decisions.
- Building meaningful relationships with others.
- Being the real you as opposed to pretending to be invincible. (No man is Superman, and no woman is Superwoman.)
- Becoming a better thinker, better listener, better friend, better parent, and better collaborator.
- Being better able to control your ego, behaviors, words, and emotions.

Please answer these questions:

*Do you buy into the power of humility and your need to embrace it? Why or why not?*

*What are seven observable behaviors that would evidence someone having humility?*

*What are seven observable behaviors that would evidence a lack of humility?*

Now ask yourself:

*Do you often do any of the humility-evidencing behaviors?*

*Do you often do any of the behaviors that evidence a lack of humility*

*So, what does that tell you?*

*And what are you going to do with that information?*

.. .. .. .. .. .. .. .. .. .. .. .. .. .. ..

Ok, let's talk about another practice that will help you have a quiet ego.

# GRATITUDE PRACTICE

Think about how many times in the last day you said any of the following words to others:

> Thank you.

> I appreciate your help.

> I appreciate the good service.

> Thank you for helping me.

> You are most kind.

> I appreciate you.

> I am grateful you are part of my life.

How many times in the last month did you write a thank you note to someone expressing words of gratitude or appreciation?

It is not surprising to me if your answer is "none or rarely."

**Gratitude Practices help you understand "It is not all about me!"**

**Gratitude Practices help you understand that you did not get to where you are by yourself.**

Many of us have not learned that expressing gratitude has powerful positive emotional consequences to both the speaker and the listener.

Practicing and showing gratitude is a way of acknowledging the positive contribution others make to you daily.

Sincerely thanking someone is evidence that you understand the important role others play in your success.

No one becomes great or happy by themselves!!

Expressing gratitude daily reminds you that it is not all about you. That will help you quiet your ego!

People who often express gratitude experience health benefits, too, including immune system improvement, lower blood pressure, and decreased stress and anxiety.

**How can you practice gratitude?**

You can practice gratitude by expressing it verbally to others.

You can write thank you notes to others.

You can send or deliver in-person a small gift with a thank you note.

You can practice gratitude for those who have passed away in your daily meditation or prayers.

You can practice gratitude in your Journal—writing down each night what you are thankful for that happened to you that day.

You can express gratitude to your family members, teachers, fellow workers, friends, bosses, and even to people you don't really know but who do something for you like holding the door or elevator open or picking up something that you dropped.

It is not that hard to say, THANK YOU!

When you express heartfelt gratitude to another person, it is highly likely they will respond positively with a smile. And in most cases, you will smile back at them automatically because that is how your body chemistry works. That feels wonderful to them and to you.

I am talking about genuine heartfelt gratitude.

I am not talking about fake gratitude.

Heartfelt gratitude will generate positive emotions in you and the other person.

Heartfelt gratitude will automatically generate a big smile in most people.

**How about right now—think about someone who recently helped you or who went out of their way to be kind to you and visualize that person and silently express gratitude to them and smile at them.**

How did that feel?

How would it feel to send them a text or email or call them and express your gratitude?

Or go see them and tell them in person?

Please do that. Why would you not do that since you now understand the power of Gratitude?

How about this? The next time you are taking a walk, and someone is walking across the street from you but coming in your direction, how about give them a wave of your hand and say: "Have a nice day."

Try it and see what happens. There is a good chance that person who you don't know at all will smile and say "You, too."

See how that feels to you.

**Practicing gratitude daily will help you have a quiet ego.**

Why? Because you are behaving in a way that says: "It is not all about me!"

**One of the most powerful things I have learned on my journey is the joy of creating in my mind and my heart positive feelings when I feel down or stressed or angry.**

Practicing Gratitude along with Mindfulness Meditation has changed my life for the better.

I am happier and more productive. I am more thankful. I appreciate the small things more. I am not so me-oriented. And I am a more kind, caring, and compassionate person. Can I improve? Yes! We all can improve all our life.

You can get to that place, too.

It is not rocket science. You do not need a college education.

# 📋 Workshop #12

In your Journal, please answer these questions:
- Why should I practice gratitude?
- What will practicing gratitude help me do or become?
- How will I daily practice gratitude?

. .. .. .. .. .. .. .. .. .. .. .. .. .. ..

**Let me emphasize again the concept of Deliberate Practice.**

I am asking you to make time each day to embrace new behaviors/practices that will help you "OWN YOUR JOURNEY."

Behavior change is the game. That is how "The Journey to Your Best Self" happens. Good intent is not enough.

**It all comes down to how you behave each day!**

Behavior change requires discipline and is made more likely by the adoption of Daily Practices that help you behave the way you desire.

Will you make mistakes? Yes. But the goal is not to make the same mistake over and over.

And it is important to start your journey by picking one or two key behaviors that are foundational building blocks for your journey.

Focus on those beginning building blocks until you are making good progress daily. Measure yourself and hold yourself accountable on a daily basis.

Recruit an Accountability Partner at work and at home. Seek their feedback and express gratitude every time for their feedback. They are helping you.

**I highly recommend you start with working on having a Quiet Ego by using the Quiet Ego Practices in this Chapter!**

# CHAPTER 5

# Become a *New Smart* Person

A key to "Own Your Journey" is changing your story about what it means to be smart.

This chapter introduces you to a new story of what it means to be smart called "New Smart."

Most of us in the United States were raised in a very competitive culture defined by survival-of-the-fittest. How was "the fittest" determined?

It starts in school at a very young age. In most cases, it is determined by the grades you get in school. The people with the highest grades are thought to be smarter than the people with the lower grades. Sound familiar?

You learned in Chapter 2 that we all are wired to seek

- Confirmation of what we believe.
- Affirmation of our ego.
- Cohesiveness of our stories.

That wiring will inhibit your long-term success and happiness because it drives behaviors and ways of thinking that inhibit your ability to learn, unlearn, and relearn at the pace of change. That in turn will inhibit your ability to continuously have good jobs in the Smart Technology Age.

I want to share with you two stories or theories that will make it easier for you to define smart in a way that will help you be a better learner and help you overcome your reactive ways of thinking that inhibit learning.

# A Growth Mindset

The first story is social psychologist Carol Dweck's theory of a growth mindset. A person with a growth mindset believes (and science backs this up), that their intelligence level is not fixed in stone at birth and that no matter your age or prior performances, you can learn and improve because your brain has plasticity — it can continuously learn.

Dweck studies human motivation and her research has shown that people with a growth mindset are better learners and more successful than those with a fixed mindset — believing their intelligence is fixed.

That is because those with a growth mindset are motivated to learn so they can move beyond mistakes, failure, and criticism. They are more likely to see effort as fruitful and obstacles as challenges to overcome rather than situations to avoid. They believe they can get better. They want to be better.

On the other hand, those with a fixed mindset are more concerned with defending what they know. They excel at the 3 D's: Deny, Defend, Deflect!

Dweck's theory of a growth mindset means that you should purge from your mind all thoughts that you are stupid or dumb or not smart.

**Everyone can learn. You can learn.**

**Everyone can get smarter. You can get smarter.**

**Everyone can improve. You can improve.**

Any past disappointing performance is not YOU forever. It is just your performance at that specific time.

If you adopt a Growth Mindset you will be better able to learn and adapt so you will have meaningful work in the Age of Smart Technology!

# 📋 Workshop #13

Please write in your Journal:

1. Your understanding of what a Growth Mindset means and how a Growth Mindset differs from a Fixed Mindset; and

2. How would a Growth Mindset help you have continuous meaningful work in the Age of Smart Technology?

OK, are you ready for a new definition of "smart" which will help you be a better thinker, a better learner, and help you quiet your ego?

.. .. .. .. .. .. .. .. .. .. .. .. .. .. ..

# NEW SMART

New Smart is a new definition of smart that reflects five principles of what it means to be a good learner in the Smart Technology Age.

New Smart is not about getting the highest grade or test score.

New Smart is not about being good at memorizing stuff.

New Smart is not about you being the smartest person in the room.

New Smart is not about you competing against other people.

Embracing the 5 New Smart Principles will help you accept a new definition of smart that optimizes your ability to learn.

Embracing New Smart will make it easier for you to be a better thinker.

Being a good critical thinker will be a necessity for the rest of your life.

## The 5 New Smart Principles

1. I'm defined not by what I know or how much I know but by the quality of my thinking, listening, relating, and collaborating.
2. My mental models are not reality; they are only my generalized stories of how my world works.
3. I am not my ideas, and I must decouple my beliefs (not values) from my ego.
4. I must be open-minded and treat my beliefs (not values) as hypothesis to be constantly tested and subject to modification by better data.
5, My mistakes and failures are opportunities to learn.

Let's explore these five principles one at a time and let's make meaning together. Let's seek to understand why adopting them will be so helpful for you the rest of your life.

## NEW SMART PRINCIPLE #1

"I'm defined not by what I know or how much I know but by the quality of my thinking, listening, relating, and collaborating."

Please write down your answers to these questions in your Journal:

- What does Principle #1 say to you?

- How can it change how you "grade" or view yourself?
- How could it change how you think, listen, relate & collaborate?
- How would adopting New Smart Principle #1 help you be a better learner?

Notice that Principle #1 does not mention being better or smarter than others. It does not mention a need to compete against others.

It really is telling you that your biggest competition will be you!

Your success will be highly dependent on how well you think, listen, collaborate, and learn.

In the Smart Technology Age what you know will be out of date very quickly because smart technology will create new and better knowledge at a very fast pace. Some thought leaders have stated that the shelf-life of knowledge will shrink to two to three years. That means you will have to constantly learn, unlearn, and relearn.

Principle #1's purpose is to free you up from defining yourself by what you think you know and help you define yourself by the quality of your thinking, listening, and learning and your ability to collaborate and continually learn. That enables you to focus on improving how you do those things.

**In your Journal, please fill in the blank:**

**I should adopt New Smart Principal #1 because: _____ .**

## NEW SMART PRINCIPLE #2

*"My mental models are not reality; they are only my generalized stories of how my world works."*

**Your mental models are your brain's stories of how your world works.**

Your brain is a suboptimal learner for reasons we discussed in Chapter 2, because

- We think our stories are correct.
- We identify with our stories. We are those stories. We seek to confirm our stories and not challenge them to make sure they are correct.
- We defend our stories if they are challenged — the 3D's. We deny, defend, and deflect.
- We do not want to admit our story is wrong—we are fearful of being wrong and looking stupid.
- We like people who agree with us.
- We rarely look for information that disconfirms our story.

Please stop and reflect.

Please reread the previous six statements one at a time, substituting the word "I" for "We" and the word "my" for "our", and honestly ask yourself: "Do I do that?"

Unless you have had great training, your answer should be:

**YES, I act that way!**

.. .. .. .. .. .. .. .. .. .. .. .. .. .

# Workshop #14

In your Journal, please write down your answers to these questions:

- **What does New Smart Principle #2 say to you?**
- **If your stories are not reality, what are they?**
- **If someone disagrees with you, do you immediately defend your view or do you ask questions to make sure you understand the other person's view and think about whether they could be correct?**

- If someone disagrees with you, do you take that personally?
- When someone disagrees with you, how often do you tell them they are correct or right?
- Why should you adopt New Smart Principal #2?

Let's take a 10–15-minute break.

OK, welcome back. Do you feel refreshed? Are you ready?

## NEW SMART PRINCIPLE #3

*"I am not my ideas, and I must decouple my beliefs (not my values) from my ego."*

If you believe you are your ideas, you won't be able to be a good learner.

If you believe you are your ideas — that they define you — then you will seek to defend your views and you will not be open-minded and you will not learn at the pace of change. You will become expert at deny-defend and deflect. That will limit your ability to continuously learn and stay employed.

New Smart Principle #3 is a big enabler. When you decouple your beliefs (not your values) from your ego you are liberated to learn — to seek out disconfirming information and to actively stress test your beliefs.

.. .. .. .. .. .. .. .. .. .. .. .. ..

# 📋 Workshop #15

Using your learnings so far, including New Smart Principles #1 and #2 above, please complete the following statements in your Journal, expressing your understanding of New Smart Principle #3:

- "I am not my ideas because my ideas are only .......?"
- "Believing that you are not your ideas would make it easier for you to do what?"
- "I must decouple my beliefs (not my values) from my ego because that would help me do what?"

. .. .. .. .. .. .. .. .. .. .. .. .. .. ..

Here are three possible answers to that exercise.

Please read them slowly one at a time. Which one makes the most sense to you? Please write it in your Journal.

- I should decouple my beliefs from my ego because that would help me: more open-minded, critique my ideas, and be willing to get input from others that would make my idea better or even convince me that my idea was not as good as I thought and that would help me not make mistakes.

- What is important to me is to have good ideas and make the right decisions, and I know from the science that I am biased toward my current ideas. Therefore, it is hard for me to see the mistakes or faults in my ideas. I need others to help me test my ideas. That means I can't be defensive and close-minded if I want to be successful. That means I need to ask others to critique my ideas.

- I am not my ideas. They are just my stories of how my world works. Other people have different stories. Their stories may be more correct than my stories because no one knows everything. Therefore, I can't be defensive when people disagree with me. I should try and understand what they are saying so I can be a better thinker and learner.

Are you beginning to see that the New Smart Principles are a pathway to becoming a better learner?

Continually being a good learner will help you stay employed in the Smart Technology Age! Ok, let's move on to New Smart Principle #4.

## NEW SMART PRINCIPLE #4

*I must be open-minded and treat my beliefs (not my values) as my tentative statements of what I believe (my hypothesis) to be constantly tested and subject to modification by better data.*

# Workshop #16

In your Journal, please write down your answers to these questions:

- What does New Smart Principle #4 say to you?
- What does the word "open-minded" mean to you?
- How would an open-minded person behave?
- How would a close-minded person behave?
- How would you test your ideas and beliefs? Would you look for information that would disconfirm your ideas? Would you ask other smart people to critique your ideas? Would you consistently read or look for relevant information on reliable Internet sources? Would you do a "Google" search on the idea or the belief you want to test — looking for expert opinions?

OK, are you ready for the last New Smart Principle?

.. .. .. .. .. .. .. .. .. .. .. .. .. ..

## NEW SMART PRINCIPLE #5

*My mistakes and failures are opportunities to learn.*

Am I crazy saying mistakes and failures are opportunities to learn?

No, I am not crazy because that is the new reality of the Smart Technology Age!

Everyone makes mistakes—even the smartest scientists, thinkers, and doctors.

The difference between good learners and poor learners is that good learners accept their mistakes as opportunities to learn so they don't make the same mistake again.

A very smart, billionaire friend of mine who built a big, successful business based on developing the best thinkers, and who is a legendary good thinker once told me that: *"We all are dumb shits!"*

The great innovator Thomas Edison said this about failure:

*"I have not failed. I've found 10,000 ways that don't work."*[5]

The great Western philosopher Socrates said:

*"I know nothing except the fact of my ignorance."*[6]

The great Eastern philosopher Confucius is reputed to have said:

*"Real knowledge is knowing the extent of one's ignorance."*[7]

What are Confucius, Socrates, Edison, and my friend saying to us?

Embracing the 5 New Smart Principles will make it easier to become a better learner and a better decision maker. That is how you become a better learner and thinker. That is how you will have meaningful work.

**You have a choice — do you want to be an Old Smart or a New Smart Person?**

## OLD SMART v. NEW SMART

| Old Smart | New Smart |
|---|---|
| Big ego | Quiet ego |
| Close mind | Open mind |
| Defend my views | Test my views |
| Listen to confirm | Listen to learn |
| Seek confirmation | Seek truth |
| I know | I'm ok with not knowing/learning |
| I tell | I ask questions |
| Mistakes are bad | Mistakes are learning opportunities |
| I am my ideas | I am not my ideas |

Here is what I truly believe: Old Smart is the New Dumb!

# 📋 Workshop #17

In your Journal, please write down your story of why adopting the 5 New Smart Principles would be a good thing for you to do.

Please grade yourself. How many of the above New Smart behaviors do you do very frequently?

And then create your daily plan for (1) reviewing the New Smart Principles, (2) visualizing behaving in a New Smart way, and (3) measuring your New Smart performance so you can hold yourself accountable and improve.

The best way to become a better person is to work daily on improving yourself and holding yourself accountable.

That is what the science of deliberate practice says. That is what great thinkers do.

That is what great athletes do. That is what great musicians do.

That is what great warriors do. That is what great learners do.

They have daily routines and practices to help them be the best they can be every day!

Carl Rogers, one of the founders of humanistic psychology said:

*"The only (person) who is educated is the (person)who has learned how to learn; the (person) who has learned how to adapt and change; the (person) who has realized that no knowledge is secure..."*[8]

*"Our goals should be to liberate ourselves — to be curious, ask questions, discover, and embrace the fact that life is change, that life is an ongoing process and a journey of learning that should never end."*[9]

.. .. .. .. .. .. .. .. .. .. .. .. .. .. .. ..

CHAPTER

# Quiet Your Mind and Your Body
## The Power of Mindfulness and Meditation

Meditation is learning how to be aware of and take control of what is going on in your body and your mind.

Mindfulness Meditation is the tool through which you can achieve awareness, calmness, and control of your inner self.

Mindfulness Meditation is also the pathway to happiness.

In his book The Art of Happiness—A Handbook for Living, The Dalai Lama says,

- *"Yes, I believe that happiness can be achieved through training the mind."*[10]
- *"(T)he greater the level of calmness of our mind, the greater our peace of mind, the greater our ability to enjoy a happy and joyful life."*[11]
- *"(I)t has to do with the development and training of your mental state, attitudes and psychological and emotional state and well-being."*[12]

The purpose of Mindfulness Meditation is for you to take control of your attention, your awareness, and your chattering monkey mind through your breathing.

One of the pioneers of Mindfulness Meditation in the United States is Jon Kabat-Zinn, a physician and meditation expert at Mass General Hospital in Boston. He describes the process this way:

*"Mindfulness is awareness, cultivated by paying attention in a sustained and particular way; on purpose, in the present moment, and non-judgmentally."*[13]

**The goal is to train your mind this way: When it wanders, do not get upset—just quickly bring the focus of your mind back to your breath or to the conversation or to what you were working on.**

**The goal is to be fully present without thinking about something else or creating your answer or critiquing yourself.**

The ancient Stoic philosophers likewise advocated daily mindfulness training. The key focus of that training was Mindfulness Meditation — being fully present in the here and now. Focusing solely on one's breath—breathing in slowly and breathing out slowly until one feels calm and in control of oneself.

Similarly modern Buddhist monk and former molecular geneticist Matthieu Ricard says:

- *"It (Happiness) requires sustained effort in training the mind and developing a set of human qualities, such as inner peace, mindfulness, and altruistic love."*[14]

- *"We look for happiness outside of ourselves when it is basically an inner state of being."*[15]

Professor Mark Williams defines mindfulness this way:

- *"You come to realize that thoughts come and go of their own accord; that you are not your thoughts.*

- *"You can watch as they appear in your mind, seemingly from thin air, and watch again as they disappear, like soap bubbles bursting.*

- *"You come to the profound understanding that thoughts and feelings (including negative ones) are transient. They come and go, and ultimately, you have a choice about whether to act on them or not."*[16]

The purpose of Mindfulness Training is to quiet your ego and stop your mind from wandering so your mind is quiet, and so you can be fully present, fully in the moment, giving your full attention to whatever you need to focus on.

Studies show that Mindfulness Training helps you spend less time thinking about you and more time focused on the task at hand, such as  listening and trying to understand others; and being fully present with another person.

Even better news is that over the past few decades, scientists have proven that **a daily Mindfulness Meditation practice over time can help you cultivate a sense of inner peace, including a quiet ego, a quiet mind, a quiet body, and a positive emotional state.**

What does that say to you?

Here is what it says to me: **"Doing Mindfulness Meditation daily will help me have a Quiet Ego, a Quiet Mind, a Quiet Body, and be more in a positive emotional state. That helps me Own My Journey and be on my Journey to Best Self!"**

THIS IS SO IMPORTANT for you to learn:

You are not automatically your thoughts! You have a choice as to whether to act them out.

You are not automatically your emotions. You have a choice as to whether to act them out.

So, how do you do Mindfulness Meditation?

# A MINDFULNESS MEDITATION PRACTICE

- Sit in a chair with your feet on the ground and your hands resting on your lap.
- At home, you can lie down if you like with your hands resting on your belly.
- Close your eyes.
- First, calm yourself by taking three to four deep breaths—breathing in slowly for a count of five and breathing out slowly for a count of five for each breath.
- Feel each breath coming up through you stomach and chest. Feel your breath going out through your nose.
- Really focus on your breath—breathing in slowly and breathing out slowly.
- **When your mind wanders (it will wander), intentionally bring your focus back to your breath. Don't get upset or mad when mind-wandering happens. It will happen. Believe me it will happen.**
- And it even happens to people who have been meditating for years. Just accept it, take a deep breath or two, and bring your focus back to your breath.
- Just let any intruding thought go.
  > Don't engage with it.
  > Don't curse at it.
  > Don't do negative self-talk.
  > Just take a deep breath and bring your focus back to your breath.

**Please do this practice for three minutes three times a day: early in the morning, at mid-day, and at night.**

After you do this practice for a few weeks, add this additional step: As you breathe in, make a big facial smile and as you breath out, slowly release your smile.

Smiling will bring you positive feelings and tell your body that this new thing you are doing is good for you and that your body can relax and go with the flow.

**Eventually increase the duration of your meditation time to five minutes three times a day.**

Again, be patient.

Your mind will wander.

It will fight you because it does not want to be tamed.

But your job is to be your own mind-tamer!

When you have made some improvement, increase your time to eight minutes per meditation session.

Then do 10 minutes.

Then you can switch to once a day if you like and do 15 minutes.

Then do 20 minutes.

It can take you months to reach 20 minutes.

That is fine. You will get positive results along the way.

Please understand that it will take time for your mind to be trained to rarely wander.

When you have been doing this a few years you will find more joy and self-progress if you up your daily meditation to 30 minutes a day everyday. And occasionally, on a weekend you can take it up to 40- 60 minutes at a time. Trust me — Mindfulness Meditation is magical.

**Stick with the program because each time you bring your wandering mind back to focusing on your breath is a**

victory. And over time your mind-wandering will decrease, and it will continue to decrease over the years as you practice Mindfulness Meditation.

Mindfulness Meditation is a key tool that will build a new way of being—a calm way of being that helps you Own Your Journey.

Mindfulness Meditation will help you have a quiet ego and a quiet mind—a mind that is still; a mind that is not talking to you a lot; a mind that is not critiquing you.

A mind that is totally focused on what you want it to be focused on: for example, your breath and eventually for example, you fully listening to someone else in a non-judgmental and non-monkey-mind way.

PLEASE TAKE A BREAK. If you can, please go outside and take a five-minute walk and practice being calm and not thinking about anything. —Just focus on breathing in and breathing out. Then come back.

# 📋 Workshop #18

IN YOUR JOURNAL, please write down your responses to the following two questions:

1. Why is Mindfulness Meditation so important for you to do?
2. When your mind inevitably wanders while practicing mindfulness, what will you do?

Below that, please rewrite the following statements and read them daily:

*I understand that Mindfulness Meditation is a daily practice.*

*I will do it every day at the same time [NOTE: Pick a time when you are highly likely to have control of that time and have no interruptions].*

*I will grade myself daily in my Journal with a checkmark for having done my meditation.*

*I will not quit!*

Why is reading these statements daily helpful? Because daily deliberate practice is how you become a BETTER YOU!

**Research has shown that daily Mindfulness Meditation helps you:**

- Control you attention
- Be aware of what is going on in your body
- Control your emotions—especially your negative emotions which can hijack your thinking
- Quiet your ego
- Reduce emotional defensiveness
- Increase positive emotions
- Enhance your thinking
- Be calm
- Reduce your fears
- Manage your emotions
- Release tension and stress in your body

**Mindfulness Meditation is one of the most powerful and reliable ways to OWN YOUR JOURNEY — your ego, your mind, your body, your thoughts, and your emotions.**

# MEDITATION RESOURCES

Online and through digital apps, you can find free guided meditations by these leading meditation professionals: Jon Kabat-Zin, Jack Kornfield, Tara Brach, Thich Nhat Hanh, Sharon Salzberg, Joan Halifax, George Mumford, and Eckhart Tolle.

I have found these resources very helpful in developing my meditation practices over the years. Choose a teacher who you find easy to listen to and with whom you can emotionally connect.

When you begin a daily Mindfulness Meditation practice, please log the frequency and number of minutes in your Journal.

Hold yourself accountable.

OK, how about you take a short break before we move on to the power of Loving-Kindness Meditation.

.. .. .. .. .. .. .. .. .. .. .. .. .

Welcome back.

## LOVING-KINDNESS MEDITATION

We all want to be loved.

To be truly loved, you must love others.

Love can be platonic (no sex) or romantic (with sex).

For our purposes throughout this book, I am talking about platonic love.

**One of the leading loving-kindness meditators in the world is Sharon Salzberg. In her book Real Love, she shared this statement by Linda Carroll:**

*"Loving yourself is holding yourself accountable to be the best you can be in life."* [17]

That quote is AWESOME!

Please read it slowly a couple of times, letting it sink into your brain and your heart.

What do you think of the quote?

You can be a good kind, caring, compassionate human being that brings comfort and joy to others, which will bring joy and comfort to you.

That is the path to meaningful relationships — caring, trusting relationships which will help you live a happy life!

# A Loving-Kindness Meditation Practice

Sharon Salzberg defines Loving-Kindness Meditation as:

*"Loving kindness is the practice of offering to oneself and others wishes to be happy, peaceful, healthy, and strong."*[18]

Loving-Kindness Meditation can focus on another person or on you.

In both situations, you begin in the same way as a Mindfulness Meditation.

- Sit or lie down in a comfortable position.
- Place your hands on your lap.
- Close your eyes.
- Relax.
- Focus on your breath.

## Loving-Kindness (for self)

Breath in deeply feeling your stomach and chest pushing your breath up your body and breathe out slowly feeling your breath release.

Do that three times to become calm and centered.

Say the following four phrases to yourself slowly, pausing for a few breaths between each one:

- **May I feel safe.**

  *Let the words sink slowly into your body, heart, and*

*mind. Then pause and let those words rest in your heart. Rest there quietly for a minute focusing on the words and then smile.*

*If your mind wanders—bring it back by saying again "May I feel safe."*

*The key here is to focus on the words you are saying. That is where you want your mind, heart, and body focused.*

- **May I be happy.**

  *Let the words sink slowly into your body, heart, and mind. Rest there quietly for a minute and then smile.*

  *If your mind wanders—bring it back by saying again "May I be happy."*

- **May I have good health.**

  *Let the words sink slowly into your body, heart, and mind. Rest there quietly for a minute and then smile.*

  *If your mind wanders—bring it back by saying again "May I have good health."*

- **May I have inner peace.**

  *Let those words sink slowly into your body, heart, and mind. Feel the calmness in your body and mind. Rest there for a minute and then smile.*

  *If your mind wanders—bring it back by saying again "May I have inner peace."*

**Please do a 3-minute Loving-Kindness Meditation now.**

After you practice this for a couple of weeks, you can add another 10 minutes to your practice and focus on sending loving-kindness to a person whom you care about deeply or a person whom you know and care about who is having hard times or health issues or a person who has helped you out a lot.

## Loving-Kindness (for others)

Begin in the same way as you Loving-Kindness Meditation (for self) but this time as you begin to focus on your breath, picture the person you want to send loving-kindness to just as if she or he was sitting in front of you. Smile at that person. A big smile. Then say to that person by name "Jim or Jane (use the person's real name) I care about you."

Then silently say the person's name before each of the following four phrases:

(Person's name), May you feel safe.

(Person's name), May you be happy.

(Person's name), May you have good health.

(Person's name), May you have inner peace.

Again, focus on the words, and if your mind wanders bring it back to the words and the face of the person to whom you are making these loving-kindness wishes.

Loving-Kindness Meditation was harder for me to learn than Mindfulness Meditation. Nonetheless, I did not give up. I was committed just like you will be.

It is part of my Daily Practices and the day I wrote this; I made loving-kindness wishes for eight people. I learned that this practice helps me have a quieter ego and it helps me be a more kind, caring, compassionate person who is not focused just on me.

**Loving-Kindness Meditation is a joyous practice.**

**It will create positive feelings in your body and heart.**

**It will help you understand why we all need others.**

**The reality is that true happiness requires positive**

emotional relationships with others who care about us and who are trustworthy allowing us to be vulnerable with them without fear.

If you would like to take a break. Please do so.

And when you are ready to bring your Best Self back to our conversation, I look forward to being with you!

# A Quiet Body

Scientists have proven that doing Mindfulness Meditation daily will help you have a Quiet Ego, a Quiet Mind, a Quiet Body, and be more in a positive emotional state. That helps you Own Your Journey & be on your Journey to Best Self!

Regarding having control over your Body, in addition to Mindfulness Meditation and Loving-Kindness Meditation, I want to introduce you to two **Deep Breathing Exercises** which likewise will help you have control over your body, your emotions and your mind.

I highly recommend doing 4-5 minutes of a Deep Breathing Exercise every morning. And during your day, do 1-2 minutes of Deep Breathing to calm your body and emotions when you feel yourself getting upset or angry or scared or out of control.

# Deep Breathing Exercises

Are you sensitive to what is going on in your body?

I bet you know when your body is all riled up.

What does that feel like?

I bet you know when you are getting angry.

I bet you know when you are fearful.

Do you feel your heart going faster?

Do you feel warmth in your face, around your ears?

Do you feel your body tightening up?

**My question for you is what do you do when you have those feelings?**

Do you let them "talk" to you until they are through?

Do those feelings stay with you a long time?

How do you take ownership of those feelings?

Do you know how to calm your body?

**The fact is you can take ownership of your body and what you are feeling. You can control your body instead of letting it control you.**

That is a huge benefit because if we learn to quiet our body, we could have far fewer incidents of acting badly and far fewer incidents of letting our emotions overcome us.

How do we take control of our body? The answer is simple:

# You Do Deep Breathing Exercises!

**Two science-based deep breathing exercises are Coherent Breathing and the United States Navy Seals' Box Breathing exercise. I have used both for years.**

I include one of them in my early morning Daily Practice every day.

**I use one of the two deep breathing exercises any time during my day when my mind or body is getting riled up. I do that to slow down my inner motor so I can be more present, calmer, and open-minded.**

Doing so enables me to think better, listen better, have better conversations, and feel happier.

Deep breathing exercises help you reach a state on inner

stillness where you can just be in the moment, calm and peaceful with a quiet ego, quiet mind, quiet body, and being in a positive emotional state.

Try a deep breathing exercise with me now.

## Coherent Breathing

» **Sit down in a comfortable position.**

» **Rest your hands on your lap.**

» **Close your eyes.**

» **Relax your body.**

» **Breathe in slowly counting to five.**

» **Breathe out slowly counting to five. Concentrate on just your breath. No self-talk.**

» **Do this for three minutes. Then work up to a minimum of five minutes once a day.**

**You can use Coherent Breathing anytime during your day to calm yourself.**

Sometimes if I catch my motor running too fast, I will stop doing what I am doing, taking deep breaths counting to five slowly on the inhale and counting to five on the exhale to become calmer.

The cool thing about Coherent Breathing is you can do it anytime during the day that you feel your body or emotions getting riled up or stressed—your face getting hotter, your heartbeat getting faster.

If any of those experiences happen during your day, it is time to take control of yourself, which you can do by practicing Coherent Breathing.

Please try it again.

How do you feel?

Did you feel calmer?

The second good breathing exercise I recommend is Box 4 Breathing, a research-based practice the U.S. Navy Seals use to manage their mental state and emotions, including fear.

## Box 4 Breathing

- » Sit down in a comfortable position.
- » Rest your hands on your lap.
- » Close your eyes.
- » Relax your body.
- » Inhale for four seconds
- » Hold your breath for four seconds
- » Exhale slowly for four seconds
- » Wait another four seconds before your next inhale.
- » Repeat for three to five minutes.

As you develop your Deep Breathing Practice you will find that you can use it as needed at work, at home, or wherever you find yourself.

Why don't you start doing these breathing exercises today?

# WORKSHOP #19

In Chapters 3- 6, you have learned about key practices that can help you become your Best Self.

Please make a list of these practices in your Journal—a master list to which you can add the practices we talk about in the next chapters.

Please take a good break before starting the next chapter.

. .. .. .. .. .. .. .. .. .. .. .. .. .. ..

# Manage Your Emotions

For many people emotions are the most misunderstood and mismanaged part of our human existence!

Emotions are intertwined within our body sensations, thinking, perceptions, decisions, and behaviors. Our body sensations can trigger emotions. Our thoughts can trigger emotions and vice versa. Gut feelings are emotional. Your brain can create emotions.

**Our reflexive (automatic) tendency is to be emotionally defensive and self-protective—we reactively deny, defend, and/or deflect (the 3 D's).**

Think about it for a minute. In the last couple of days, did you have a conversation where your reacted automatically in a 3 D's manner?

Our emotions are created by our hormones and by the chemical neurotransmitters in our brain. Our emotions feel automatic, influencing our responses often before we're even aware of something to respond to.

One reason this happens is because we subconsciously pick up signals from other people's tone, facial expressions, body language, emotions, and behaviors.

For example, an emotional response might be triggered by another person's:

- Lack of eye contact
- Lack of attention
- Interrupting us when we're speaking
- Negative attitude
- Specific words
- Loudness
- Rudeness

And the other person's emotions can be triggered by you doing one or more of those things, and all of it can happen outside of our conscious awareness and seemingly out of our control.

Professor Jane Dutton is one of the three Founders of The Center for Positive Organizations at the University of Michigan, and the author of the wonderful book: *Energize your Workplace: How to Build and Sustain High Quality Connections.* She is a very kind, caring person that role models what she teaches.

Her research shows that people interpret 50% of what we're trying to communicate from our body language and 38% from our tone. Our words are communicating only 7% of the story.

Wow — please read that paragraph again. Are you surprised? I bet you thought your words have the most impact. I did. I was wrong!

Most of us have never been taught how to generate positive emotions and how to manage negative emotions.

**Understanding how to generate positive emotions and how to manage your negative emotions is MISSION CRITICAL in the Smart Technology Age.**

Why?

**Because many of the jobs that will be available to you will require positive emotional engagement with other people.**

Emotional excellence will be the real difference between you and smart technology.

The good news is that you can learn how to manage your emotions. You can learn how to generate positive emotions and how to manage negative emotions.

Many people automatically let their feelings control or drive their behaviors like there is an automatic link between the two. That does not have to be the result.

You can break that auto-reflexive response by using the techniques we are going to discuss in this chapter.

All of us have fears. Sometimes our fears are justified. They are a warning signal. For example, they might indicate that you are not in a safe place or that someone wants to harm you or is harming you. In those cases, an automatic fight or flight response will be necessary. I am not talking about that kind of fear.

I am talking about everyday stressors that can generate a high level of fear even when you're not at risk for physical harm.

That is the kind of fear that comes about when you are insecure or when you are afraid to speak up because you may be wrong or when you are afraid of looking bad or not being liked. Or when you are working with or for a disrespectful tyrant or mean person.

**The renowned psychologist Abraham Maslow stated: An individual engages in learning "to the extent that he (or she) is not crippled by fear, to the extent he (or she) feels safe enough to dare."[19]**

Science tells us that positive emotions enable better health, open-mindedness, better thinking, better decision making, better listening, better collaborating, better problem solving, and more meaningful relationships, well-being, and happiness.

Negative emotions tend to inhibit those desired results in many cases.

Everyone is insecure, anxious, and fearful. The difference between us is the extent of those feelings and our abilities to manage those feelings.

So, how can you manage your unwanted negative emotions?

First, you must be aware of them. Be sensitive to your heart rate or body temperature increasing. Be sensitive to your perspiration or your mouth becoming drier. Those messages tell you that something is happening inside of you that you need to focus on.

Second, try and label your emotion. For example, I am feeling insecure, angry, or fearful or scared or I am being very cautious.

Then you need to slow your body down and not reflexively react without thinking about how you should act. The following exercises can help.

# MANAGE YOUR NEGATIVE EMOTIONS

# The Power of Pause

Before you react take a few deep breaths and pause. Do a minute or two of Coherent Breathing or Box 4 Breathing, which we discussed in the previous chapter. Then you can proceed with the following additional exercises.

### Stop and Think

Try to override your automatic emotional response through slow, logical thinking. Try to reduce the magnitude of the bad feeling by probing where it came from. What is going on that ignited your fear?

For example, ask to yourself:

- "Why do I feel insecure or fearful?"
- "Am I misreading him or her?"
- "Do I need to ask some questions to understand what is going on."

## Look Down on Yourself

Imagine you are a fly on the wall and look down on yourself. Get out of your head and look at the situation as if you are not in the situation. Ask yourself why are you reacting that way? What is a better way to react?

## Think About Positive Memories

Think about your loved ones or very happy times. Feel the happiness. Smile. That will release positive emotions that will calm you down. Then you will be more in control of yourself and more likely to respond appropriately.

## Do Positive Self-Talk Using Your Name

- "Ed, calm down my man!
- "Ed, take a deep breath or two.
- "Ed, slow down and respond in a manner that you will feel good about.
- "Ed don't respond—ask some questions to make sure you know what the person meant."

## The If-Then Tool

This is an approach you can use if you are heading into a difficult meeting or conversation. Ask yourself beforehand:

- "What could go wrong?"

*You may have a couple of thoughts. Visualize that happening.*

- "If that happened, how should I react?"

*Visualize responding appropriately. Be specific.*

- "If X happens, I will do Y."

*Then if it happens do as you planned without losing your emotional balance.*

# 📋 Workshop #20

In Your Journal, please copy and complete the following prompts:

- **Tomorrow, I will start using the following tools to manage my negative emotions: _____.**

- **I want to manage my negative emotions because: _____.**

- **This is how I will try and control my negative emotions: _____.**

OK. Now that you have some tools for managing negative emotions, do you know how to generate positive emotions?

It's easy compared to keeping your negative emotions under control. Here are some ways to generate positive emotions.

## GENERATING POSITIVE EMOTIONS

1. Smile more. You can't smile enough. Smile at yourself.

2. Laugh more.

3. Be kind.

4. Visualize your kind, caring loved ones.

5. Say "Thank you" often — express gratitude.

6. Take a break and text someone a positive message giving thanks or wishing them well.

7. Seek micro-joys. Go outside for a few minutes and focus on Mother Nature—or relish a coffee break. Don't think at all. Just be calm and totally focused on the joy and stillness of the moment.

8. Take a five-minute stillness break in a soft cushioned chair or sit outside and take some deep breaths and be completely calm and quiet inside your body. Just being in the moment being completely still enjoying your inner peace.

.. .. .. .. .. .. .. .. .. .. .. .. .. ..

# 📋 Workshop #21

**In your Journal, please write down how you are going to start generating positive emotions. Which of the eight tools will you adopt?**

Your goal and my goal should be to go out in our world every day in the best emotional state we can be in under our circumstances and try to maintain or improve that positive state as we go through our day.

That means we need to maintain control or ownership of our thoughts, emotions, and behaviors as best we can throughout our day.

Do you now understand how important your emotions are in determining how you behave, learn, and relate to others?

Recall that the goal of this book is to help you **Own Your Journey** so you can have **meaningful work, meaningful** relationships, and happiness in the Age of Smart Technology & Radical Change.

Our ability to do that is highly dependent on how well we manage ourselves—how well we take ownership of our ego, mind, body, and emotions and how well we connect and relate with other human beings.

All of that is enhanced through generating positive emotions and managing negative emotions.

So, as we leave this chapter, I do so giving you a BIG SMILE.

.. .. .. .. .. .. .. .. .. .. .. .. .. .. ..

# Workshop #22

In your Journal, please answer these questions:

1. I must focus more on managing my emotions because?

2. I will use these Tools (make your list) daily to generate more positive emotions?

3. I will use these Tools to manage my negative emotions?

4. My key learnings from this Chapter are?

. .. .. .. .. .. .. .. .. .. .. .. .. .. ..

# Own Your Words and Behaviors

One purpose of this book is to help you understand that every day you have lots of choices—more than you think.

And two of those choices are that you can take ownership of your words and your behaviors.

Yes, there are some things you can't control.

Recall the Serenity Prayer: *"God, give me the Serenity to accept the things I cannot change, the Courage to change the things I can, and the wisdom to know the difference."*[20]

But let's focus on the many choices you do have.

In earlier chapters, we discussed how you can generate positive emotions. Is that something that you can control? **Yes!**

We also discussed how you can manage your negative emotions and not let them overtake you. Do you have the choice to manage your negative emotions and not let them overtake you? **Yes!**

Do you also have a choice about whether you have a Big Ego or a Quiet Ego? **Yes!**

Do you have a choice about whether you have a chatterbox "monkey-mind" or a Quiet Mind? **Yes!**

Do you have a choice about which words come out of your mouth? **Yes!**

Do you have a choice as to how you behave? **Yes**

Every day you have the power to choose how you behave in every human interaction.

# BEHAVIORAL CHOICES

- Your attitude.
- Your actions.
- The words you use.
- Your body language.
- Whether to be kind or not.
- Whether you are fully present or not.
- How you respond to the other person.
- Whether you really listen or not.
- Whether you pause and think before you react.
- Whether you follow the 5 New Smart Principles.
- Whether you come to the conversation with a quiet ego, a quiet mind, a quiet body, and a positive emotional state.

You have the choice to OWN YOUR JOURNEY!

# OWN YOUR WORDS

**In your daily conversations, do you consciously choose the words you use, or do you just start talking and words just automatically come out?**

Most of us respond automatically.

We say the first think that pops up in our head. Have you ever done that? Sure, you have. We all do it unless we have learned not to.

**The key is to pause and reflect. Pause and think before you speak.**

**Think about the impact your words may have.**

Many people respond without asking questions to make sure they understood what the other person meant. And many people do not paraphrase what they hear back to the speaker and ask, "Is this what you meant?"

Most of us talk without thinking about how our words and behaviors will impact others.

The wrong words, or the wrong tone, or the wrong body language can cause negative, defensive responses by the other person. The wrong behaviors can do the same.

We all need to understand that the words we use, our body language, our facial expressions, our tone of voice, whether we make eye contact, and whether we are multitasking send messages to the other person.

**Remember the Power of the Pause. Don't be on autopilot.**

Pause, reflect, and think and ask clarifying questions before you speak or respond.

I am a big fan of Roshi Joan Halifax's work. She is a Buddhist monk who oversees Upaya Institute and Zen Center in Santa Fe, New Mexico. Her life story is amazing and inspirational. She role models everything positive that we are talking about in this book and more.

**In her book Standing at the Edge she offered Five Gateways of Speech:**

1. Is it true?
2. Is it kind?
3. Is it beneficial?
4. Is it necessary?
5. Is it the right time?[21]

The Five Gateways of Speech are questions that she recommends we ask ourselves before we respond to the person or the situation. To do that we have to PAUSE and REFLECT!

With her *Five Gateways of Speech* Roshi Joan Halifax is asking us to take ownership of our speech — our words and to respect the human dignity of the other person and to not do harm intentionally or unintentionally.

**Her Five Gateways of Speech require us to focus on:**

- **The purpose/intent of our words.**
- **Our motives.**
- **The possible unintended impacts that our words could have on the other person.**

Eknath Easwaran, a leading advocate of Eastern philosophy, said in his wonderful book "Words To Live By" that:

*"(T)here are three kinds of violence: one, through our deeds: two, through our words; and three, through our thoughts."* [22]

# 📋 Workshop #23

**In your Journal, please write down what the Five Gateways of Speech mean to you.**

Why wouldn't you want to put Roshi Joan's Five Gateways of Speech on a 3 x 5 card and carry it around with you and read it many times every day before you converse with others?

The Power of Pause and the Five Gateways of Speech are two powerful tools that if used often can help you manage your Words and your Behaviors so that you can make better decisions, build better relationships, be a better learner, be a better listener, and be a better person.

Let's move on to Behaviors.

# MANAGE YOUR BEHAVIORS

Another big choice you have is how you behave!

**What are behaviors? Behaviors are:**

- Observable actions or inactions that send messages or impact the other person.
- How you make public your intentions, your values, and your way of being.
- Your daily observable actions or inactions.
- How people understand and judge you.
- What people react to.
- Behaviors are how you evidence or operationalize or put into practice a Quiet Ego, a Quiet Mind, a Quiet Body, and a positive or negative emotional state.

Does that make sense to you?

**Behaviors can have positive results, and behaviors can create negative results. It depends on your motives, intent, and actions. It depends on your CHOICES!**

You can train yourself to increase your good behaviors and decrease your bad behaviors by drilling down and identifying the sub-behaviors of each.

For example, what sub-behaviors would evidence that you are fully present and truly listening to what the other person is saying and what behaviors would evidence you are not doing that?

We are going to do that exercise in the next chapter.

**Keep this in mind. If you unintentionally behave badly and possibly hurt someone, reach out and make amends. Apologize and ask for their forgiveness.**

I remember an incident in my early years as a leader when a young man walked past me in the hallway, and I was so self-absorbed that I did not acknowledge his existence. When I got back to my office, the young man's boss—one of my direct reports—called me very upset.

He said, "My star young data analyst is working on his resume because you did not acknowledge him when he said 'hello' to you this morning and that meant you did not like him. So he was going to leave the company because he would never be promoted to a higher rank since you did not like him."

I said, "WOW! I don't remember seeing him."

My direct report asked, "Well, what are you going to do about it? This young man is a superstar and my best analyst."

What would you have done?

Well, I went to the young man's cubicle and asked to speak with him.

Notice I went to the young man's cubicle. He said "Ok" and I sat down in a chair by his desk and faced him and I apologized to him and asked what I could do to make this right for him. He said he wanted to work with me on a big project to which I agreed.

**Notice I did not make excuses. I took ownership of my behavior. I apologized. I asked him how I could make amends. I agreed to his request. And I did what I said I would do.**

And that young man was so outstanding that he worked with me on many big projects, and he got well-earned promotions. He went on to become the successful CEO of a public company.

If his boss hadn't called me out, we would have lost a superstar performer. Not because I was evil or mean but because I was self-absorbed.

Why did I share that story? What can you learn from it?

**Do you remember the statement I made at the beginning of the book?**

**The statement that "your biggest competition going forward will not be others — it will be you!"**

**Your success in life is highly dependent upon you taking ownership of you — what you can control — what you can improve — who you want to be.**

. .. .. .. .. .. .. .. .. .. .. .. .. .. ..

# 📋 Workshop #24

**In your Journal, please explain why your biggest competition will be you.**

**Why is this important?**

Because your success and happiness in the Smart Technology Age is highly dependent on the quality of the human relationships you have inside and outside of work.

That is why you need to "rewire" yourself so you can bring your "Best Self" to each conversation and each human engagement.

Do you want to Own Your Journey?

Do you want to be on The Journey to Best Self?

Do you want to have good meaningful work?

Do you want to have good meaningful relationships?

Do you want to be happy?

*Then "Take Ownership" of You and:*

> Be really present totally in the now, with a quiet ego, a quiet mind, a quiet body, and a positive emotional state.

> Be a force of positivity not negativity.

> Be kind. Speak kindly. Act kindly.

> Express gratitude often.

> Smile often.

> Seek to truly understand the other person.

> Manage your words, behaviors, and emotions.

> Live the Golden Rule: Do unto others as you wish them to do unto you.

> Don't strive to be respected, to be important, to be better than others; strive to be your Best Self.

> Think right and act right.

> Don't raise your voice against others.

> Don't stare at people.

> Don't clench your fist when you are talking with another.

> Don't lean your body into a person—respect their space.

> Don't cross your arms when you are listening to someone.

> Don't verbally or physically attack another person unless you are in danger.

> Don't tell another person you know how they feel because you don't.

> Respect the human dignity of the other person.

> Do no harm.

> Own your mistakes, and if possible, make it right with the other person.

> Don't lie.

> Don't be rude.

> Do not ridicule anyone.

> Do not give others the power to control you.

I invite you to take the above list of behaviors and type it on a piece of paper and put that piece of paper in a clear folder and read that list every morning, periodically during your day and at night and grade yourself each night looking for where you made mistakes or behaved badly.

And then the next day or sooner make amends with others.

To "OWN YOUR JOURNEY" requires you to create your personal story that enables the right mindset, the right behaviors, the right words, the right thinking, the right emotions, the right listening, and the right kinds of communication with others.

.. .. .. .. .. .. .. .. .. .. .. .. .. .. ..

# Workshop #25

I invite you to reread this Chapter and then reflect on everything up this point.

Behaviors are how you operationalize — put into practice the learnings of this book. Good intent is not enough. Your success in the Age of Smart Technology and Radical Change will be highly dependent upon how you behave.

Now in your Journal, please create a list called "**My Daily Behavioral Intentions**" — your new story of how you want to behave and express yourself daily.

Start your list with these words: "I will behave this way every day." Once you have made your list, I recommend

**you put in your Journal and read it first thing every morning visualizing how you want to behave each new day.**

There is no rush. Take your time and think about your choices. Visualize how you want to be with others. Visualize saying the specific words you want to start using.

Please take your time. This is so important.

.. .. .. .. .. .. .. .. .. .. .. .. .. .. ..

I hope you did the exercise. What did your list say?

Every year I rewrite my Daily Intentions. Here is my list. I am not saying my list is better than yours. I am not saying my words are what you should use. I am sharing to give you a feel for what I am asking you to do. I am sharing to stimulate your thinking because I have used this exercise many times with leaders and students.

I want you to get very specific and choose measurable observable behaviors so you can hold yourself accountable.

# Ed's 2023 Daily Behavioral Intentions:

1. Meditate at least 30 minutes in the morning.
2. Do deep breathing exercises in the morning and during the day.
3. Be really -really present — in the now.
4. Be a kind, caring, compassionate, courageous person.
5. Say: "Thank you" often.
6. Smile often.
7. Be a force of positivity not a force of negativity.
8. Manage my negative emotions.
9. Generate positive emotions.
10. Manage my mind.
11. Be calm — stay calm — take deep breathes.

12. Really, really listen.

13. Be in the moment — not the past or the future.

14. Ask — don't tell.

15. Do not allow others to define me.

16. Don't immediately react — pause and reflect.

17. Accept what I can't change.

18. Don't give others the power over me.

19. Use positive words — such as:

Please — Thank you — I care about you — I am grateful you are part of my life — Please forgive me — I forgive you — I am so sorry — I am here for you- You will be in my prayers — You are a good person — You are right — I was wrong- I apologize — You are a good person.

Now please go back and revise your list to make it very simple, direct, and operational since you now understand what I mean by "Daily Behavioral Intentions."

**CHAPTER**

# Reflective Listening

## 📋 Workshop #26:

### Please answer these questions in your Journal:

Have you recently had a conversation with someone who was multitasking while you were talking?

How did that feel?

Do you think the person could multitask and really understand what you were saying?

Have you recently had a conversation with a person who interrupted you to put forth their ideas before you were finished?

How did that feel?

Do you think the person was trying to understand what you were saying or showing you how smart they are?

Have you had a recent conversation with someone in which you multitasked?

Do you think you could truly understand the other person while you were doing something else?

How do you think the other person felt when you were not fully present and listening?

Have you had a recent conversation in which you interrupted the speaker before they were through talking?

Why did you do that?

Did you think about how the speaker would feel if you interrupted them?

How would you feel if someone interrupted you in the middle of your statement?

How often do you tell the speaker your response without first asking questions to make sure you understood what they were saying?

. .. .. .. .. .. .. .. .. .. .. .. .. ..

Listening is all about trying to understand what the other person is saying, and many times you will have to ask the person questions to figure that out.

Do you remember our conversation about how we are wired?

We are wired to seek confirmation of what we believe and affirmation of our ego — essentially, we are looking to confirm our views from the stories we have created.

So, how do you make sure you understand another person when you are wired to automatically interpret their words in a way that makes sense to you as opposed to trying to truly understand what the words mean to them?

Good listening skills are going to be even more important in the Smart Machine Age because they are key to continually learning. Recall that we all must continually learn new things faster than we ever have before because smart technology will continue to create new knowledge and new ways of working faster than we have ever experienced.

In the Age of Smart Technology and Radical Change, much work will be done in small teams to optimize making the right decisions and optimizing how to create new and better products and services for your customers or patients. That means that Reflective Listening will be a key behavior and tool.

**I have told many business leaders that success in this new Era will be highly dependent upon "the quality of the conversations in the workplace."**

**Reflective Listening is mission critical to having high quality making-meaning conversations with others.**

Seek to understand and explore by asking good questions and listening with a non-judgmental open mind will be key behaviors.

Good listening skills involves asking questions to make sure you understand what the other person is saying.

**"Ed, this is what I heard you say.... Am I hearing you correctly?"**

**"Ed, I do not understand what you meant when you said this... Could you please help me understand what you meant?"**

**"Ed, thank you for your explanation. This is what I think.... What am I missing? Where am I wrong?**

We all must become faster, better thinkers and faster, better learners.

We must continually learn new jobs and new ways of working. Learn — unlearn and relearn at the speed of change. That is how you and I will stay relevant workwise!

That means people who excel at collaborating with others will do better than people who do not excel at collaborating.

**My psychology mentor, Dr. Lyle Bourne, Jr., taught me that *"All learning comes from conversations with yourself (deep reflection) or with others."* That is reflective listening.**

**Reflective listening is enabled by having a quiet ego, a quiet mind, a quiet body, and a positive emotional state. Reflective Listening is enabled by a New Smart Mindset.**

The best listeners try to get the right or best answer regardless of their view or opinion.

They are motivated to learn more than they are motivated to defend their views. They are motivated to get the best result, the best answer not their answer.

Reflective listeners are not automatic, fast responders.

They PAUSE, reflect, and ask questions to confirm that they heard the speaker correctly before responding. They seek to understand the other person.

Reflective listeners often say something like:

**"Jim, let me tell you what I heard and please tell me what I am missing or where I am wrong."**

**"Jim, this is what I heard... Was that what you meant?"**

A speaker can help initiate reflective listening by asking the listener:

- "What did you hear?"
- "What made sense to you?"
- "What did not make sense to you?"
- "What am I missing?"
- "Is there a better approach?"
- "What concerns you?"

Reflective listening is not a competition.

Reflective listening is all about learning, making meaning with other people, and coming to the best conclusion.

Reflective listening is being fully present with a quiet mind seeking to really understand what the other person is saying.

Reflective listening is not about creating your answer while the speaker is talking.

Reflective listening is not about showing everyone how smart are you.

Here is a Getting Ready to Listen Reflectively Checklist © in my *Humility Is the New Smart* book: [23]

- "Is my mind clear (calm, quiet)? If not, take several deep, slow breaths."
- "Am I calm emotionally? If not, take a few more deep breaths, focusing on breathing in for four seconds and very, very slowly breathing out for four seconds."
- "Say to yourself a couple of times:
  > "I am not my ideas."
  > "It's not all about me."
  > "Don't be defensive."
  > "Ask questions before telling."
  > "Don't interrupt."
  > "Stay focused."
  > "Critique ideas, not people"
  > "Listen to understand, not to confirm."

# Workshop #27

Over my decades consulting with clients about Reflective Listening, I have observed the characteristics of two kinds of listeners in a work environment: Reflective Listeners and Bad Listeners.

Please honestly grade yourself on each listening behavior. What do you usually do?

| Reflective Listeners | Bad Listeners |
|---|---|
| Focus on the speaker's words | Thinking of my responses |
| Be Open minded | Be Closed minded |
| Have a Quiet mind | Have a Wandering mind |
| Have a Quiet body | Show Negative body language |
| Calm speaking tones | Raised or loud voices |
| Seek to understand | Seek to validate my views |
| Be Non-defensive | Be Defensive |
| Ask questions to understand | Ask questions to confirm |
| Seek the best results | Seek my desired result |
| Don't rush to judgment | Quick to judge |
| Listen to learn | Listen to confirm my beliefs |
| Seek to make meaning with others | Want others to agree with me |
| Critique the idea | Critique the Person |
| Be Fully present | Multitask |
| Don't' interrupt | Interrupt |
| Say "Yes, and" | Say "Yes, but" |
| Collaborate | Compete |

It only takes a few of the bad listener characteristics to be a Bad Listener.

On the other hand, a Reflective Listener must exhibit most of the reflective listener characteristics to be successful.

Renowned Humanistic psychologist Carl R. Rogers, one of the leading authorities on people-centric conversations, described what it is was like to truly be heard by others:

*"I like to be heard. ....These persons have heard me without judging me, diagnosing me, appraising me, evaluating me. They have just listened and clarified and responded to me.....(When) someone really hears you without passing judgment on you,... without trying to mold you, it feels damn good!"* [24]

Reflective listening and seeking to understand another person can be evidence that you respect and care about them. That is how you begin to build caring, trusting relationships. That is how excel in the Age of Smart Technology!

. .. .. .. .. .. .. .. .. .. .. .. .. ..

# 🗒 Workshop #28

**Here's an exercise for your Journal:**

**Make believe you have been asked to teach people how to be a Reflective Listener. What story will you tell them?**

. .. .. .. .. .. .. .. .. .. .. .. .. ..

**CHAPTER**

# Manage How You Think

## 📋 Workshop #29

In your Journal, please answer these questions:

When do you think?

Why do you think?

How do you think?

.. .. .. .. .. .. .. .. .. .. .. .. .. ..

I have asked hundreds of executives the "How do you think" question and only one person has ever given me an answer that made sense. Yes, only one.

Some people answer, "Stuff just pops up in my head."

Others answer: "It just happens" or "I don't know. I just do it."

There are different types of thinking. For example: Critical Thinking, Creative Thinking, Innovative Thinking, Moral Thinking, and Emergent Thinking.

I want to focus on Critical Thinking because it will be a key skill to help you learn, and to help you make the right decisions and right personal choices in Age of Smart Technology where new knowledge will be continuously created at a very fast pace.

99

In other words, I want you to have the foundational thinking skills or approaches which help you to learn -unlearn and relearn at the speed of change.

Earlier I stated that the shelf-life of most knowledge will become shorter and shorter. You will have to constantly look for new data/facts all the time to make sure your decisions and way of working are still good ways.

**So, how do you learn to be a good Critical Thinker?**

> **Critical Thinking is not listening to and automatically doing what your "monkey mind" says.**

> **Critical Thinking is not biased thinking — it is not confirmation thinking.**

> **Critical Thinking is not accepting the first thing that comes into your mind.**

> **Critical Thinking is not believing that everything you believe is correct.**

> **Critical Thinking is not automatically taking advice from a friend.**

The lack of Critical Thinking in our Society is one of the reasons we have so much divisiveness. Too many people who are not good Critical Thinkers think they have the correct and the only correct answers.

Critical thinking is all about testing your beliefs and ideas. It requires you to ask yourself:

> **Why do I believe this?**

> **What facts propel me to believe this?**

> **What facts would disconfirm what I believe?**

> **Have I looked for that disconfirming information?**

Thinking critically is how scientists operate. They challenge their views and ideas by intentionally looking for information that contradicts what they believe.

They do this by seeking feedback from people who have different views and by taking steps to overcome the natural tendency to seek confirming data.

**We all have that tendency to seek confirmation of what we believe and interpret things in ways that coincide with our existing stories of how our world works.**

Critical thinking, on the other hand, requires you to be open-minded and constantly challenge your thinking to make sure it is still good.

Why should you learn to think deliberately and critically? Because you want to:

- Make the best life decisions you can make.
- Do good work and have good work.
- Be able to quickly learn new skills and stay employed.
- Have good relationships—the kind that require understanding others and helping them achieve their goals.
- Optimize happiness and minimize making big mistakes at work and in life.

# 📋 Workshop #30

**Recall a recent time when you paused to think deeply, deliberately, and critically:**

- What were you thinking about and why?
- Were you trying to make a decision that was hard?
- Were you trying to learn something new?
- Were you trying to fix something that was broken?
- Were you trying to help someone figure out what to do?
- Were you trying to come up with a better way of doing your work?
- Were you trying to figure out how to be a better parent, friend, or teammate?

- How did you engage in that kind of thinking—what exactly did you do?
- What if any questions did you ask yourself?

.. .. .. .. .. .. .. .. .. .. .. .. .. .. ..

Without thinking critically, how do you know you are right or correct?

Without thinking critically and critically evaluating the choices, how do you know you are making the right decisions?

Critical thinking is how you make the best decisions.

Critical thinking is not accepting or doing the first thing that pops up in your head unless you are in harm's way or unless you are deciding whether to drink orange juice or grapefruit juice as an example.

**In all cases Critical Thinking requires you to unpack the reasons — the facts that underly your belief.**

**"Why do I believe this?"**

**"What facts do I have that support my belief?**

**Do I have enough data/facts? That depends on the downsides of being wrong. The bigger the downside, the surer you need to be that you are the doing the right thing.**

In many cases, critical thinking requires you to go find more information.

Maybe your question has been dealt with by other smart people. Look on-line or talk in person with smart people who have more experience, and don't be satisfied with one person's response. Depending on the importance of the decision you will want multiple confirmations from qualified people — not people who know little about the question or idea.

Thinking critically should be your way of thinking about everything that has real consequences in your life — at home and at work and out in the world.

**When you need to think deliberately, use these questions:**

- **What am I trying to do?**
- **Why am I trying to do that? What is my purpose or goal?**
- **What facts or evidence do I have that supports what I want to do?**
- **What facts or data would disconfirm what I want to do?**
- **What do I not know that I need to know?**
- **How do I get that information?**
- **Have I looked hard for disconfirming information?**
- **Have I reduced any big financial, physical, emotional, and reputational downsides to zero?**

The biggest inhibitors to being a good deliberate critical thinker are laziness, your ego, your fears, and being a poor listener.

**Good deliberate critical thinkers approach thinking with a Quiet Ego, a Quiet Mind, a Quiet Body, a positive emotional state, and a New Smart Mindset. And they are good Reflective Listeners.**

# CRITICAL THINKING TOOLS

## THE 5 NEW SMART PRINCIPLES©

1. I'm defined not by what I know or how much I know but by the quality of my thinking, listening, relating, and collaborating

2. My mental models are not reality—they are only my generalized stories of how my world works.

3. I am not my ideas, and I must decouple my beliefs (not values) from my ego.

4. I must be open-minded and treat my beliefs (not values) as hypothesis to be constantly tested and subject to modification by better data.

5. My mistakes and failures are opportunities to learn.

Accepting and using these 5 New Smart Principles should help you quiet your ego, be more open-minded, be more willing and able to look for disconfirming information, and not accept the first positive answer you find.

## CRITICAL THINKING PURPOSES & QUESTIONS

- To make good, reasoned decisions based on good facts not on hopes or guesses or little data.
- To clearly define the issue or the question or the problem.
- To analyze one's thinking.
  › What do I think?
  › Why do I believe that?
  › What assumptions am I making?
  › What facts must be true for my thought or idea to be good?
  › What facts do I have?
  › Do I have enough facts or data that supports my view?
  › What facts would disprove my belief or idea?
  › Have I searched enough for facts that would say my idea or belief is wrong?
  › Do I have enough credible evidence to make my decision?

> › Who disagrees with my position, answer, or potential course of action? Why do they disagree? Have I taken their views into consideration?
> › If I do X, what could happen? The Good? The Bad?
> › Have I mitigated all big downsides—the big risks?

## THE 5 WHYS: ROOT CAUSE ANALYSIS

- What is the real problem?
- What is the real cause of the problem?

The answers to those questions can be explored by using the 5 Whys: asking a serious of "Whys" for each answer until you get to the core foundational answer.

For example: Why did that happen? Because of X. Why did X happen? Because of Y... and so one.

## GARY KLEIN'S PREMORTEM TOOL

Gary Klein is a brilliant leading psychology researcher who has written four of my favorite books on thinking. His PreMortem Tool is a great tool.

It requires that you take the following steps before you take any important action or make a big or important decision in your work life or your personal life:

1. After you make an important decision but before you act on it — STOP and visualize what failure would look like. Yes, what could happen if you are wrong. Visualize what failure looks like. What could go wrong?

2. Then make a list of all the possible reasons that such a failure could occur.

3. Think deeply about how to mitigate or prevent those reasons for happening. In other words, figure out how to reduce the risks.

4. Then review your decision — your course of action.

Have you reduced the likelihood of bad results? Are you comfortable proceeding?

This is a very good tool because it demonstrates that critical thinking is about deliberating on the pros and cons of your potential actions and your behaviors before you act or make decisions and making the best decisions you can make.

## U.S. ARMY AFTER ACTION REVIEW (AAR)

The AAR is a helpful tool for critical thinking and learning that was created by the U.S. Army but is now widely used by businesses and other organizations and individuals.

I use it. It is simple and it works. Its purpose is to help you learn from your mistakes and not make the same mistake twice.

You can use it daily to review your performance in meetings and situations with others at work, and in your personal life.

The AAR consists of six questions:

What happened?

Why did it happen?

What worked?

What did not work?

Why did it not work?

What should I do differently next time?

CHAPTER

# The Power of Otherness

In this chapter you will learn how to actively cultivate meaningful, caring, trusting relationships with others.

Let's think about why you need other people ("Others").

Our need for Others is as old as our human history. Our ancestors going back to the hunter-gatherer days survived because they cooperated and built friendships with others based on mutual trust. Social cooperation was how people survived the longest. Survivors trusted each other, helped each other, and cared about each other.

**Despite our cultural fixation with "survivor of the fittest," our history and modern science have shown that cooperation with others is not only innate but key to our health, well-being, and success. No one is happy by themself.**

## Workshop #31:

In your Journal, please identify the people in your life who have:

- Helped you along your way.
- Given you opportunities.
- Opened doors for you.

- Offered you a hand when you were down.
- Been there for you in difficult times.
- Cared for you when you were ill.
- Listens to you in a caring non-judgmental manner.

We all need a few trusted Others who care deeply about us and will do everything legally possible to help us be happy.

So how do you create those types of relationships?

**One answer is the Golden Rule: *Do unto others as you would have them do unto you.***

You do it by behaving in ways that inspire people to care about and trust you. You don't do it by sucking up to people. You do it by demonstrating that you truly care about the other person, and you respect their human dignity, and you will keep their "secrets" confidential, and you will be there for them as needed. You must earn their trust.

You bring your whole self to the table — not just your good self. You have the courage to share your fears, your mistakes, your challenges, and your problems. It takes time to build those kinds of relationships. You are not trying to have many "soul friends" — you just need 2 or 3.

**To build meaningful, caring, trusting relation-ships-friendships with other people requires you to honestly behave in kind, caring, compassionate, and non-manipulative ways with others.**

If you are a true friend, you are always truthful and never try to fake your feelings to get something from others. You do no harm.

**To develop and maintain Otherness depends on whether you bring your Best Self or your self-centered self to the**

situation. Being self-centered — "it is all about me" is not conducive to building caring trusting friendships.

Many of us did not grow up with the best models of meaningful, caring, trusting relationships with others. Nonetheless, we all must learn how to better cultivate and maintain them in our work and personal lives

Trust is so important in relationships. It takes time to build that trust.

**Saying "I trust you" is not good enough. Words are cheap. Trust is evidenced by behaviors.**

How the other person behaves with you is as important as how you behave with him or her?

How many people do you trust with telling them your most vulnerable feelings or the most fearful things that you worry about or feel insecure about?

**We must remember that:**
- We all are human beings.
- We all breathe in, and we all breathe out.
- We all want to live, to be, and to do.
- We all want to love and be loved.
- We all want to be happy.
- We all want not to suffer.
- We all want to feel safe.
- We all want our human dignity respected.
- We all want to provide for ourselves and our family.
- We all want to wake up tomorrow morning.
- We all want joy.
- We all need others to help us be our Best Self.

- Unfortunately, we all are not born into wealth.
- Unfortunately, we all don't have the same opportunities.
- We all are still due respect, human dignity, and the opportunity to be all we can be.

**Building meaningful, caring, trusting relationships with people at work and in your personal life depends on cultivating the behaviors and practices discussed in earlier chapters. For example:**

- Own Your Journey!
- Work on being your Best Self.
- Expressing gratitude to others.
- Managing your ego, mind, body, emotions, words, and behaviors.
- Be a Reflective Listener.
- Connecting and relating to others in an emotionally positive way.

All the great ancient philosophies and great religions embrace Otherness directly or indirectly through stated values or virtues such as self-control, humility, compassion, generosity, empathy, kindness, gratitude, doing no harm, courage, integrity, respect, wisdom, justice, forgiveness, trustworthiness, veracity, and reciprocity.

**Not only do we need others to comfort and help us in difficult times, and to share our joy in good times, but also, we need others to help us think and learn at our best.**

You have learned that in the Smart Technology Age we all must continually learn, unlearn, and relearn.

You have also learned that your innate wiring can inhibit your learning.

This Chapter's purpose is for you to learn that your success in life will be highly dependent upon you building caring, trusting relationships with Others. Those types of relationships will enable you to collaborate better and to think at your highest levels and learn at the speed of change.

We all need others to help us:

- See what we can't see.
- Test our beliefs.
- Give us honest feedback.
- Help us learn.

**How do you cultivate Otherness?** It all depends upon how you behave with others and how others emotionally feel about you:

- Do they feel safe with you?
- Can they trust you?
- Do you truly care about them and respect them as a unique person?
- Will you be there for them when they need help?

# HIGH-QUALITY MAKING-MEANING CONVERSATIONS

Building meaningful, caring, trusting relationships is also key to having what I call High-Quality Making-Meaning Conversations.

A High-Quality Making-Meaning Conversation is a conversation (with another person or a conversation with a small group of people) where all parties are seeking to understand each other, and each person is seeking to be understood by others in a caring, trusting, non-competitive manner that is respectful of everyone's human dignity.

It is not a conversation characterized by advocacy or self-promotion or competition.

It is a conversation where everyone's perspective is respectfully considered or where people try hard with an open-mind and a kind heart to make meaning together trying to understand each other.

**It is only through making meaning together that we can truly understand what others mean to communicate and that requires understanding the definitions of key words as well as the values, sentiments, and reasons underlying those words.**

Those types of conversations are magical. It takes integrity, patience, and everyone bringing their Best Self to the conversation with the right purpose and mindset.

Mutual trust is key to those conversations because trust enables people to feel safe enough to have fearless, vulnerable, and honest conversations because they know you care about them and won't hurt them.

I am sharing now—this is not about me—I have been very fortunate to experience with various consulting clients those types of conversations with people who are on their personal journey to their best selves, and the conversations are truly MAGICAL. The group ends up with decisions or judgments that are so different and better than they expected

Building caring, trusting relationships, and having High-Quality Making-Meaning Conversations with Others is a process and is totally dependent upon how you behave. It requires a quiet ego (Chapter 4 & 5), a quiet mind and body (Chapter 7), managing your emotions (Chapter 8), owning your words and behaviors (Chapter 9), and reflective listening (Chapter 10).

# 📋 Workshop #32

In your Journal, please answer these questions:

1. What does the word "caring" mean to you?

2. What behaviors would "tell" someone that you care about them?

3. What kind of body language would indicate that you care?

4. What tone of voice would indicate that you care?

5. What role does Reflective Listening play in building caring, trusting relationships?

6. What words would evidence you care?

7. Who do you think truly cares about you? (Name them)

   • Why do you think that person cares about you?

   • How do they behave towards you?

8. What behaviors would tell you that someone does not truly care about you?

.. .. .. .. .. .. .. .. .. .. .. .. .. ..

# 📋 Workshop #33

## Caring, Trusting Behaviors

Now, reflect on whether the following behaviors would evidence that someone truly cares about you.

Please grade yourself on the extent that you do these behaviors in conversations with others using this 5 — point scale:

1 =Very rarely; 2 = Rarely; 3 = Sometimes;
4 = Often; 5 = Most of the time

- Being fully present with no multitasking.
- Smiling at the person a lot.
- Maintaining eye contact with the other.
- Exhibiting positive body language toward the other.
- Speaking with a positive caring tone.
- Being nonjudgmental.
- Seeking to truly understand the other's situation.
- Reflectively listening.
- Not trying to solve the other's problem or giving them an answer.
- Respecting their human dignity.
- Not saying, "I know how you feel," because only they know that.
- Asking questions to help you explore their feelings and the meaning of the words they use.

.. .. .. .. .. .. .. .. .. .. .. .. .. .. ..

**You can't assume another person has the same defini-tion of words that you have.**

Would you agree that a person who cares about someone should want to understand them?

**Asking questions is far more effective than telling.**

First make sure you have listened to the person's situation and asked enough questions that you feel comfortable giving advice or feedback. If the person wants advice, then use words like "I would consider" or "I would think about" to start your answer.

And would you agree that a person must bring a caring, trusting self to the conversation to truly understand the other person?

How would you feel if a person truly listened to you with a non-judgmental open mind and asked you questions with the sole purpose of clearly trying to understand you and your situation?

How would you feel if the person did the above and then said to you, "I am here for you. I care deeply about you. What can I do?"

**Remember that Otherness is a two-way street.**

**That means reciprocity is necessary.**

**That means you must behave in a caring, trusting manner.**

**Otherness depends highly upon the YOU that you bring to the conversation. Do you bring a Quiet Ego? Quiet Mind? Quiet Body? Positive Emotional State?**

Building caring trusting relationships takes time, effort, and is highly dependent on you bringing your Best Self to the table.

Without trust people will be fearful of being honest with you. People will wonder about your motives.

Trust is not possible if you compete with a person or lie to a person, or you try to make the other person look bad.

# Workshop #34:

In your Journal, please complete the following exercises:

- List seven behaviors which that would indicate you care about another person and seven that would indicate the opposite.

- List seven behaviors which would indicate you are trustworthy and seven that would indicate the opposite.

- Choose three behaviors that you want to improve and three behaviors you want to eliminate.

Our Society today is unfortunately divisive, hierarchal, and based on a survival of the fittest mentality. That makes building Caring, Trusting Relationships even more important. We all need Others to help us be the best we can be. We all need good friends to be happy!

.. .. .. .. .. .. .. .. .. .. .. .. ..

CHAPTER

# Make It Happen!
## Create Your "Take Ownership of You Plan"

You have been on quite a journey through the first eleven chapters. I applaud your work.

**The purpose of this book was to help you learn and adopt proven practices and ways of thinking that will increase the probability that you will have "Meaningful Work & Happiness in the Age of Smart Technology and Radical Change."**

We all will be in a race with technology. We will all have to learn how to add value in ways that smart technology can't — keeping in mind that technology will continue to advance and get smarter and smarter meaning that we will have to continue to get better and better to stay ahead of the technology.

It is highly likely that you will have several different jobs during your lifetime. The younger you are the more jobs you will likely have.

It is highly likely that your job will require emotional intelligence and positive emotional engagement with others.

**This book has given you the tools that will help you to think, listen, relate, collaborate, adapt, and learn better. It has given you the tools to have a Quiet Ego, a Quiet Mind, a Quiet Body, and a Positive Emotional way of being.**

It has given you the tools to manage your emotions — generating positive emotions and managing your negative emotions. It has given you the tools to build Caring, Trusting Relationships.

It has given you tools to **OWN YOUR WORK JOURNEY** as well as your life journey.

If you have not started working on improving you, now is time for you to start working daily on improving YOU!

Before creating your Plan, I recommend that you review your Journal and the "Workshops" that you have done as you read this book. They should have illuminated areas where you need to improve.

Secondly, most people find it very helpful to have one or two Accountability Partners — a trusted relative, friend, or spouse who will check in with you each day to see how you are doing and will hold you accountable for doing your Daily Practices.

Then, review the lists, tools, and the practices in the book.

Keep in mind that you need to develop the skills to learn, unlearn and relearn at the speed of technological advancement.

Remember your biggest competition is YOU — not Others.

## "My Daily Behavioral Intentions"
## &
## "My Daily Practices"

I recommend that your beginning Plan take at least 15-20 minutes of time in the early morning and 15 minutes before you go to sleep. That time should be spent solely on improving you. I am not talking about technical skills now.

It is best to do your Daily Behavioral Intentions and rehearse your Daily Practices first thing in the morning right after you wake up when it is more peaceful, and when you have more control over your time. You need a quiet calm place to do this work. It needs to be uninterruptable — except for an emergency.

Then, it is best for you to take time at night before you go to sleep to grade your performance daily and to write down in your Journal how you are going to improve.

# Workshop #35:

## Create Your "Daily Behavioral Intentions"

Your Daily Behavioral Intentions are how you want to behave each day.

What observable behaviors will help you become your "Best Self"?

Make a list of the key behaviors that you want to do every day. I would in the beginning keep your list short — 7 key behaviors" Please take some time now to choose your Daily Behavioral Intentions.

This is a very important step for you. Please reread your Journal entries.

What seven behaviors would be good building blocks for you because you feel they will help you become a better you?

Then, the first thing each morning as part of your Daily Practices read your list of Daily Behavioral Intentions and visualize doing each behavior.

# My Beginning Daily Deliberate Practices

## Your Beginning Early Morning Practice (15 minutes)

### 3-4 minutes: Gratitude Practice

In your words give "Thanks" for this day and the opportunity to be here (to be alive) and state that you will use this day wisely to do good today (or insert your positive purposeful words).

And then visualize individually and express your gratitude and love to the key people by name who helped you get to where you are.

### 3 minutes: The Box 4 Deep Breathing Practice

1. Lye or sit down in a comfortable position.
2. Rest your hands on your lap.
3. Close your eyes.
4. Relax your body.
5. Then inhale for 4 seconds
6. Then hold your breath for 4 seconds
7. Then exhale slowly for 4 seconds
8. Then do not breathe for 4 seconds
9. Then do steps 5-8 for a total of 3 minutes

### 3-4 minutes: Mindfulness Meditation Practice

1. Sit in a chair with your feet on the ground and your hands resting on your lap. At home, you can lie down if you like with your hands resting on your belly.
2. Close your eyes.
3. First, calm yourself by taking 3-4 deep breaths — breathing in slowly counting 1 to 5 and breathing out slowly counting 1 to 5 for each breath.

4. Then breathe in slowly focusing on your breath and then breathe out slowly focusing on your breath. Feel each breath going in and coming out. Feel each breath coming up through you stomach and chest. Feel your breath going out through your nose. Really focus on your breath — breathing in slowly and breathing out slowly.

When your mind wanders, and it will wander, intentionally bring your focus back to your breath. Don't get upset or get mad when that happens. It will happen. Believe me it will happen.

And it even happens occasionally to people who have been meditating for years. Just accept it, take a deep breath or two and bring your focus back to your breath.

Just let the "intruding thought" go.

Don't engage.

Don't curse at it.

Don't do negative self-talk.

### 4-minutes: Review Your 7 Daily Behavioral Intentions

Read your list slowly visualizing behaving the way you desire to behave.

### Your Night-time Review (15 minutes)

Every night review yourself. Focus on your seven key behaviors.

Mentally visualize how you behaved. When you did not behave in the way you wanted, visualize doing it the appropriate way.

Grade yourself every day in your Journal. Seek feedback from your Accountability Partner.

Each night create your list of "do overs" to rectify as soon as possible — did you behave in ways for which you need to apologize?

Did you hurt or embarrass someone, or did you make them look bad or did you come on too strong? Make amends as soon as possible. Own your behaviors.

End your nightly practice by Meditating for 2-3 minutes and doing your Gratitude Practice.

**Do this for 2 weeks everyday and keep a Journal to grade yourself and make notes.**

*My Beginning Daily Deliberate Behavior Improvement Practice*

After two weeks doing the above beginning practices, you should pick one key behavior that you need to improve. Keep doing your morning and nightly practices as above. This is a new task:

*Below are some key behaviors to consider:*

1. Humility
2. Reflective listening
3. Generating positive emotions
4. Managing negative emotions
5. Being mindful — fully present with a quiet mind and quiet body
6. Connecting with others in positive emotional ways

Once you pick your behavior to improve, please review the book chapter where that behavior was highlighted.

*Then do the following:*

Make a list — define six granular observable sub-behaviors that would evidence the desired behavior and define six granular observable sub-behaviors that would evidence the lack of the desired behavior. Really drill down to granular observable behaviors. Ask your Accountability Partner to critique your choices. Are they observable? Will they achieve your desired behavior?

After getting that feedback then rewrite your list of 6 observable behaviors that will evidence the desired behavior and 6 observable behaviors that would evidence the lack of the desired behavior.

Then everyday work on behaving in the way you want to behave.

You should consider putting those lists on a small 3 x 5 card which you can carry around with you daily to remind you how you want to behave and not behave.

Then grade yourself during the day when you have a break or at lunch or at the end of your day. At night review your grades and try to understand what triggered the bad behaviors and visualize how you should have acted and write down in your Journal how you will act differently tomorrow.

Get feedback daily if you can from your Accountability Partner because he or she probably saw you behave that day.

You will keep working on that behavior until you are most of the time doing the desired behavior.

When you reach that point you choose another behavior and do the same process.

## I want to leave you with some life-long behavioral goals:

– Be kind to others.

– Be respectful of others.

– Do no harm.

– *Respect the human dignity of every person.*

– *Do not intentionally demean or embarrass any person.*

– *Do not ridicule any person.*

– *Be a positive person not a negative person.*

– *Express gratitude often.*

– *Be a good learner.*

– *Develop a quiet ego.*

– *Be a reflective listener.*

– *Manage your emotions.*

– *Manage your mind and body.*

– *Ask questions to learn.*

– *Don't make the same mistake twice.*

– *Be someone that others can trust.*

– *Be someone that helps others.*

– *Compete only against yourself.*

– *Don't waste your time being envious of others — spend your time becoming your Best Self.*

– *Give gratitude every day for having that day. Use it wisely. It could be your last day.*

– *Your biggest competition is YOU.*

– *Live the Golden Rule.*

– *Keep in mind the Serenity Prayer.*

# Conclusion

## "Meaningful Work & Happiness in the Age of Smart Technology and Radical Change."

I hope this book has shown you that it all comes down to CHOICE. You have a choice about how you behave and how you think, listen, learn, and relate to others.

You have a choice as to whether to develop a Quiet Ego, a Quiet Mind, a Quiet Body, and Manage your Emotions.

You have a choice as to whether you want to own your Words and Behaviors.

You have a choice as to whether you want to be a *New Smart* person or stay an *Old Smart* Person.

We live in a time of Societal Divisiveness and Radical Change. You have choices as to how you deal with that reality.

There will be people who will double down on their selfishness, greed, power, and big egos.

There will be people who are overwhelmed by the challenges and who will have much suffering.

There will be courageous virtuous people who have become or are on their Journey to Best Self who will continuously have meaningful work and happiness while helping others. The purpose of this book is to increase the probabilities that you will be that kind of person.

I wrote this book for every person 18 years old or older who wants to:

- Have meaningful work and live a happy life.

- Be successful and respected as a unique human being.
- Not be left behind or overwhelmed by the pace of continual technological, economic, and social change in an era of radical change, social divisiveness, and climate change.
- Not be automated out of a job by artificial intelligence or smart robots within the coming decades.

Achieving those goals is highly dependent upon how you think, listen, behave, manage your emotions, relate to, and collaborate with others, and learn, unlearn, and relearn at the speed of change.

You will live in the most disruptive domestic time since the Great Depression. What got you here won't get you there in this new era of constant change and upheaval.

**The foundational building block of *Own Your Work Journey* is you becoming your *Best Self*.**

**That is "The Path to Meaningful Work & Happiness in the Age of Smart Technology & Radical Change."**

To be your Best Self requires you to take control of your life by taking ownership of your ego, your mind, your emotions, your body, and your words and behaviors so you can continuously learn and adapt to the pace of change.

That will enable you to continually think and listen better, make better decisions, generate positive emotions, manage your negative emotions, be more productive, and have positive relationships with others. Those are the skills that are necessary to navigate and have a happy life in this new era.

I invite you to be on the Journey to your Best Self.

I invite you to ask 2 or 3 of your friends to join you on this Journey and meet for an hour every week sharing your progress, challenges, and learnings with each other and helping each other achieve your goals. Create your *Journey to Best Self Team*.

I want to leave you with these additional thoughts:

**Be a Courageous Learner – Always Looking for Ways to Be Better & Do Better.**

- TAKE OWNERSHIP of YOU!
- Prioritize your goals and actions.
- Be a proactive "can-do" person – each day is an opportunity.
- Define and seek to achieve your purposes.
- Go out into the world with a quiet mind, quiet ego, positive emotional state etc.
- Look for surprises. Learn from surprises.
- Look for approaches different than yours. Learn from others.
- Seek to learn everyday!
- Listen to Podcasts of very reputable, successful people.
- Take free Courses in your areas of interest on Coursera.
- Find people who think differently than you and seek to understand what they believe and whether they have ideas or approaches that would help you.
- Ask exploratory questions: "Why?" "What if?" "Why not?"
- Embrace differences and try to understand them and then decide how that impacts you.
- Bring your Best Self to the World every day!
- Be a kind, caring, compassionate, courageous quiet ego person every day!

I thank you for your engagement.

I wish you all the BEST on your Journey!

~Ed

www.ownyourworkjourney.com

# Index of Practices and Tools

# Endnotes

1. Hess, *MAKE IT HAPPEN! Six Tools for Success*, p. 17 (Marietta, GA. EDH Ltd. 2000)

2. Cameron, *POSITIVELY ENERGIZING LEADERSHIP*, p. 83 (Oakland, CA. Berrett-Koehler Publishers, Inc. 2021)

3. Peterson & Seligman, *CHARACTER STRENGTHS and VIRTUES*, p. 462 (New York. Values in Action Institute 2004)

4. P.Z. Myers, "The Mediocrity Principle" in Brockman, *This Will Make You Smarter,* p.6.

5. Hess, *LEARN or DIE*, p. 136, n. 2 (New York. Columbia University Press, 2014)

6. Hess & Ludwig, *HUMILITY IS the NEW SMART*, p. 47-48 (Oakland CA. Berrett-Koehler Publishers, Inc. ©Edward D. Hess 2017)

7. Ibid.

8. Kirschenbaum and Henderson, The Carl Rogers Reader; Edward D. Hess, *Hyper-Learning: How to Adapt to the Speed of Change*, p. 66 (Oakland, CA Berrett-Koehler Publishers, Inc, © Edward D. Hess 2020).

9. Ibid.

10. His Holiness The Dalai Lama and Howard C. Cutler, M.D., *A Handbook For Living: THE ART OF HAPPINESS*, p. 4 (New York, Riverhead Books, ©1998 by HH Dalai Lama and Howard C. Cutler, MD)

11. Ibid pp. 15 & 16

12. Ibid p. 295

13. Jon Kabat-Zinn, *Mindfulness for Beginners*, p. 1 (Boulder, CO, Sounds True, Inc. 2012)

14. Matthieu Ricard, *Happiness*, pp. 7 &8 (New York, Little Brown & Company, ©2003 NiL editions, Paris)

15. Ibid p. 33

16. Mark Williams and Danny Penman, *Mindfulness: An Eight-Week Plan for Finding Peace in a Frantic World*, p. 83 (New York: Rodale, 2011)

17. Sharon Salzberg, *REAL LOVE*, p. 11 (New York, Flatiron Books, 2017 ©Sharon Salzberg)

18. Ibid, p. 18

19. Hess & Ludwig, p. 156

20. Robertson, *STOICISM AND THE ART OF HAPPINESS*, p. 14 (The McGraw-Hill Companies, Inc. 2017 ©Donald Robertson)

21. Halifax, *STANDING AT THE EDGE*, p. 165 (New York, Flatiron Books 2018 ©Joan Halifax)

22. Easwaran, *WORDS TO LIVE BY*, p. 114 (Tomales, CA, Nilgiri Press 1990 © The Blue Mountain Center of Meditation)

23. Hess & Ludwig, p. 120

24. Carl R. Rogers, *A WAY of BEING*, p. 12 (New York, Houghton Mifflin Company 1980)

# About the Author

Edward D. Hess is a Professor Emeritus of Business Administration; Batten Faculty Fellow & Batten Executive-in-Residence Emeritus at the Darden School of Business, University of Virginia.

He recieved his B.S. from the University of Florida; his J.D. from the University of Virginia and his L.L.M. from New York University

Professor Hess spent more than 20 years in the business world as a senior executive at Warburg Paribas Becker, Boettcher & Company, the Robert M. Bass Group and Arthur Andersen.

He joined academia in 2002 as an Adjunct Professor of Organization and Management at the Goizueta School of Business at Emory University where he taught in the Business Undergraduate and MBA Programs and was the Founder and Executive Director of both "The Center for Entrepreneurship and Corporate Growth" and "The Values-Based Leadership Institute."

In 2007, he joined the faculty of the Darden Graduate School of Business as Professor of Business Administration and the first Batten Executive-in- Residence. He has taught in the MBA & EMBA Programs; in over 21 Executive Education programs at Darden, IESE (Barcelona), the Indian School of Business, Georgia Tech; and AVT Denmark.

He is the author of 14 other books and well over 160 practitioner articles and over 60 Darden cases, etc. dealing with innovation and learning cultures, systems, and processes. He has been the guest on many Podcasts globally.

The common theme of his work is high individual and organizational performance.

Six of his books were published by Academic Presses: Cambridge University Press; Stanford University Press; and Columbia Business School Publishing.

His book *Smart Growth* was named a Top 25 business book in 2010 by Inc. Magazine and was awarded the Wachovia Award for Research Excellence. His book *Learn or Die* was an Amazon best seller and was awarded the Well Fargo Award for Research Excellence. His recent best-selling book is Hess & Ludwig, *Humility Is the New Smart: Rethinking Human Excellence in the Smart Machine Age* (Berrett-Koehler, 2017).

Hess's work has appeared in *Fortune* magazine, *European Business Review, HBR, SHRM, Fast Company, WIRED, Forbes, INC., Huffington Post, Washington Post, Business Week*, the *Financial Times*, and in more than 400 other global media publications as well as on CNBC Squawk Box, Fox Business News with Maria Bartiroma, Big Think, WSJ Radio, Bloomberg Radio with Kathleen Hayes, Dow Jones Radio, MSNBC Radio, Business Insider, and Wharton Radio.

His recent book *Hyper-Learning: How to Adapt to the Speed of Change* (Berrett-Koehler, 2020) sets forth a cognitive, emotional, and behavioral model designed to enable the highest levels of human adaptation and performance in the Digital Age.

He has consulted regularly for 20 years with corporations and governmental agencies. He also does executive coaching in the areas of Organizational Transformation and Human Development.

He is a Certified "Marshall Goldsmith Stakeholder Centered Coaching Coach."

His website is www.edhess.org

Made in United States
Orlando, FL
02 March 2023